EARLY AMERICAN HISTORY

NORSEMEN BEFORE COLUMBUS

By

J. Kr. Tornöe

UNIVERSITETSFORLAGET

UNIVERSITETSFORLAGET

Distribution offices

NORWAY
BLINDERN, OSLO 3

UNITED KINGDOM
16, PALL MALL
LONDON S. W. 1

UNITED STATES
BOX 142
BOSTON 13, MASS.

PRINTED IN NORWAY BY
HARALD LYCHE & CO., DRAMMEN

NORTH ATLANTIC LIBRARY

No. 1. Morris Davis: *Iceland extends its fisheries limits.*

« 2. J. Kr. Tornöe: *Early American history.*

« 3. J. F. West: *The history of the Faeroe Islands* (in preparation).

Contents

List of maps 6

Foreword 7

Introductory 9

The Viking Ships 11

Bjarne's Voyage 19
Bjarne's discovery of America 20
Sailing directions, times, and distances, from the
Hauksbok 32
Some well-known voyages 35
A hypothetical reconstruction 38
The saga about Bjarne's voyage. Fact or fiction?.. .. 43
Aftermath 46

Leiv's Discovery of Vineland 49
Comment on Leiv Eiriksson's expedition to Vineland 52
Leiv's sun observation in Falmouth.. 64
The wild grapes in Vineland 69
Conclusions 73

Thorvald's Expedition 76
Comment on Thorvald's exploits 78

Thorfinn Karlsefne's Exploration of America.. .. 85
Comment on Karlsefne's exploration 90
Where was Hop? 112
Karlsefne's defense plan 114
Karlsefne's dispositions along the American coast .. 116

Bibliography 122

Folding map 128

List of Maps

Map. 1. Showing the routes taken by Bjarne Herjulfsson, Leiv Eiriksson, Thorvald Eiriksson, and Thorfinn Karlsefne on their voyages to America and back to Greenland. p. 39.

Map. 2. Showing the probable courses taken by Bjarne, Leiv and Karlsefne across the northeastern end of the Strait of Belle Isle. p. 57.

Map. 3. The location of Scatari off Cape Breton with the routes of the Vineland voyages. p. 61.

Map. 4. Martha's Vineyard and Falmouth, with the bearings for Eyktarstad and Dagmálastad. p. 68.

Map. 5. Plymouth Bay and Harbor. p. 83.

Map. 6. The routes taken by the Vineland voyagers around Cape Cod, and past Block Island, and the location of Leiv's *Budir*. p. 96.

Map. 7. The approach to Manhattan through Long Island Sound and the probable courses of the voyagers. p. 103.

Map. 8. The location of *Hop* to the north of the mouth of the Patuxent River. p. 113.

Foreword

Not many years ago the main question under discussion with respect to the Vineland voyages was whether they took place or not. Today, of course, we know that the voyages were undertaken; archeological discoveries, such as those of Helge Ingstad in Newfoundland, and evidence of historical records offer proof that the Norsemen sailed to America and settled there for a time.

When I began my research in this subject in about 1930, as a hobby, I, like many others, accepted the view of Fridtjof Nansen and Gustav Storm that the sagas were mainly fiction. But extensive investigation later led me to agree with G. M. Gathorne-Hardy that they are based on fact. I was able, by tracing the courses sailed by the Norsemen back and forth between America and Greenland, to give the locations and limits of Helluland, Markland, and Vineland; these have been described in my previous work, *Lysstreif over Noregsveldets Historie* (Meddelelser nr. 56, *Norges Svalbard- og Ishavs-Undersökelser;* Summary in English, p. 207).

Since about 1945 I have been studying details in these lands, following strictly the text in the saga. Along the American coast I have succeeded in locating and identifying one by one, here a name, there an island, a promontory, a fjord, and other features described in the old records.

There is, of course, an element of fiction in the saga, as there is in all the history of that time, but it is not difficult to distinguish the fantasy from the fact. There is certainly no reason to attribute so much of the records to fiction as many authors have done. I intend to publish an evaluation of the sagas, which I maintain were written at about the time of Are Frode (1068-1148), in a later work, which, it is hoped, will come to the attention of teachers of early American history.

My English versions of the extracts from the sagas which appear in the present work, are based on the excellent translations of G. M. Gathorne-Hardy and Einar Haugen.

This book represents the first part of my manuscript. The second part, which concerns American history from Leiv Eiriksson to Columbus, deals with some expeditions to the American coast and an suggestion that Columbus was on a voyage in the Arctic. Publication of the second part, under the title *The Early Voyages to America,* is now in progress.

I should like to express my gratitude to the Nansen Foundation for financial support toward the costs of printing this book.

J. KR. T.

Introductory

This study is devoted mainly to the voyages of four men, Bjarne Herjulfsson, Leiv Eiriksson, Thorvald Eiriksson and Thorfinn Karlsefne. Claims are asserted in respect of the much debated location of certain scenes of Viking activity, such as Leiv's *Budir,* and of the courses sailed by these explorers. It will be shown that Bjarne discovered America 15 years before Leiv, though for perfectly simple reasons, which I shall explain, he did not set foot on the continent.

The claims are based on the sagas. There have been times during my thirty years of study of this subject when I have been tempted to swim with the current of opinion that has borne so many students into calm waters where they can construct cautious and negative theories in safety. Many excellent works on the subject have been published by eminent scholars, but so few of these — and this is important — have been seamen. Too often the seemingly unlikely has been so closely identified with the impossible that the best evidence available, that to be adduced from the sagas, has been held inadmissible or even remoulded to fit a preconceived idea.

We are fortunate indeed to have any written evidence at all from a time when, at any rate in the far north, scientific recording was almost unknown. The data offered in the sagas cover matters that were believed to be noteworthy at the time, but there are often tantalizing lacunae that must be filled, if possible, by resorting to other evidence.

I propose to interpret the accounts of the voyages of these Viking leaders in a manner that has not hitherto been attempted. Before undertaking a more detailed examination of the voyages, I shall give a short description of the ships in which these men sailed, their rigging and potentialities, and the means by which their captains navigated them without instruments.

Thereafter an explanation will be given of the manner in which the passage of time was recorded. These details must be borne in mind throughout the study; failure to attach sufficient importance to them can lead and has led to misunderstandings, and to erroneous location of places referred to in the sagas.

The Viking Ships

In order to obtain a clear view of these voyages, it is essential to understand the speed of which these ships were capable.

In my book *Lysstreif over Noregsveldets Historie*,[1] I have made some estimates regarding the distances actually sailed in 24 hours by such ships.

What one notes first (Pls. I, II, IV) about the Viking ships is that they were especially constructed for speed. They were rather shallow boats, the Gokstad ship being of only five feet draft. Owing to this the friction of the sea was relatively slight, which means, too, that they offered little lateral resistance and were liable to make leeway. As a countermeasure to this defect, they were fitted with a very deep keel along the entire length of the vessel. The keel of the Gokstad ship, for example, is 20 inches in depth from the boat's bottom. This kind of keel, naturally, also made a ship's motion in rough seas much more steady, by cutting down the rolling. The Viking ships were lighter than any other vessels of the same size. They were constructed of thin planking fitted on to wooden ribs. Since they were also open boats, they were naturally considerably lighter than the types of ships constructed in later ages. This obviously allowed the Viking ships to sail much faster than later vessels.

To suppose that the speed of the Viking ships was only five to six knots is quite erroneous. The speediest of the

[1] Oslo, 1944, pp. 66-67.

old boats was the long ship, i.e., the warship, faster because longer and relatively narrower than the merchant ships. All these boats were so constructed that, as soon as they got good way on, they tended to be lifted up in the water; the greater the speed, the more they rose or 'planed' — rather like modern speed-boats. This was possible on account of their lightness in proportion to the beam. That they were thus able to rise up in the water while sailing is one of the reasons for the unusual speed they attained.

Though I have not had the opportunity to sail on any of the reconstructed Viking ships, I have had a good deal of experience with sailing boats on the sea in my youth. The boats we used were built and rigged very similarly to the Viking ships, even though our craft were much smaller. Quite frequently, while out on the sea, our boats were so sluggish with fish and equipment that we were on the verge of foundering. Often only a few inches of freeboard remained, and waves threatened to fill the boat. In conditions like these we would set sail as quickly as possible, for once we had begun sailing, we knew we were out of danger. The boat lay over to leeward and sped over the waves easily and comfortably.

While sailing it was important to have the boat trimmed well. If too much of the catch and gear had been placed in the forepart, the boat seemed unable to rise in the waves, but, as it were, stumbled forward. Then the speed was minimal. If the weight had been placed too far aft, the boat seemed to hang in the water by the stern. But the captain knew his boat well and soon sensed what had to be done. In a small boat it was sufficient to shift one man forward or aft. But in a larger boat some of the catch and gear had to be moved till the vessel was correctly trimmed. It was quite easy to tell the difference when under sail. So it must have been with the Viking ships. And it is a well-known fact that larger fishing boats of the kind in which I gained experience attained sailing speeds of up to 10 or 12 knots. The larger ships of those earlier times could obviously sail even more rapidly.

12

The deck-covered ships of later times became altogether too heavy to skip over the waves in the manner of the Viking ships. However, the ships with decks could take a very large amount of sail. They could literally break their way through the waves, and thus attain good speed. And because they were constructed more strongly, these ships of later times surpassed the more primitive Viking ships in everything but speed.

In 1893 Captain Magnus Andersen sailed from Norway to America in a boat constructed exactly like a Viking ship. It was in fact a facsimile of the Gokstad ship (Pl. I), which was excavated in 1880. The vessel was about 70 feet in length, and displaced some 32 tons. Captain Andersen wrote a book about his voyage in the ship, which he named *Viking*. When he reached the American coast, he met many sailing vessels, and got a good chance to test the sailing capacity of his *Viking* against the more modern sailing ships. He relates that to his great surprise his *Viking* kept pace with most of them, even when sailing on the wind.[2]

Among the many vessels encountered by the *Viking* was a large fourmasted schooner with which Andersen was in contact during an entire night. Every time they went on to the next tack they met the schooner, which had to hold off to leeward. When morning arrived, the wind slackened off. By then both the schooner and many other ships were situated to leeward of the *Viking*.

The captain of the schooner and his wife paid a visit to Andersen at the fair in Chicago. He told Andersen how he had marveled at the behavior of the *Viking* with its primitive sailing equipment. He thought that the *Viking* lay deep in the water — from 8 to 10 feet. When he was told that the draft was barely 5 feet, his wife exclaimed: 'Now you see how right I was when I contended that if it had been 10 feet deep it could not have sailed so brilliantly over the shoals in Nantucket Sound.' But the captain learned the secret of the mystery when he was told that the *Viking* had a 20-inch keel under its entire length.

[2] Magnus Andersen: *Vikingefærden*, pp. 232-33, 256-58.

The shape of the Viking ships was perfect for speed. Magnus Andersen told me that he had an opportunity to compare drawings of the bottom of the Viking ships with drawings of the bottoms of some of the fastest clipper ships, and the designs basically corresponded.

The *Viking*'s log shows that on the journey over to America she had an average speed of 10 knots during an entire day and night. During shorter periods the log shows speeds of 11 knots. There was a northwest gale and the sea was very rough. Not many ships would do better. Even the large four-masted schooner was left behind by the *Viking*. For the contest they had a headwind, yet, even with this evidence available many commentators tell us that the Viking ships could not sail on the wind. Frederick J. Pohl, for instance, writes: [3] '... Viking ships of the eleventh century sailed effectively only with following or quartering winds.' Or again: [4] 'Having only one square sail, which was without a boom, the ship could not sail close to the wind. She could make material progress toward her goal only with a following or quartering wind. The maximum speed of such a viking ship under most favorable conditions of wind and water was only slightly above 6 miles, or 6¼ knots [*sic*], according to Professor Hovgaard.'

This is a misunderstanding. However, it is not only Pohl who has been of this opinion, but most of the scholars who have written about the Vineland voyages. This point of view has prevented them from understanding what the saga tells.

Those who are familiar with the squaresail know that this rig can be as good as any for windward work, even for tacking purposes. The only difference between squaresails and other sails, when combating headwinds, is that the squaresail of the kind referred to must be lowered when the ship is going over to another tack, and then hoisted again on the other side of the ship. Suppose a ship is sailing with a headwind, with the sheet on the port side, and it

[3] Frederik J. Pohl, *The Lost Discovery*, 1952, p. 109.
[4] Ibid., p. 16.

14

becomes necessary to take another tack, and lay the ship over to the other side. On turning the ship on to the other tack the sail is quickly lowered. Then the crew bring the whole sail ahead of the mast and hoist it again while fastening it forward and sheeting it to starboard. A trained crew can do this in half a minute. This is the only difficulty with the squaresail in a headwind.

The saga relates that Leiv Eiriksson had to tack (*beita*) when he rescued Thore and his crew from their shipwreck. Thorfinn Karlsefne had to beat to windward when he sailed up to the coast of Nova Scotia from the north. There is little doubt that the Viking ships, handled as they were with supreme skill, were handy to windward.

An attempt to deduce what kind of sail the ships had, and to explain its potentialities may help to clear up other misunderstandings.

We have two types of squaresail in Norway. Most likely the oldest type is the one that is used in North Norway up to our time (see Pl. IV a, p. 49). The sail is almost square, with a long spar (*rå*) on top. It is this type of sail that the Vikings are usually considered to have used.

The other, long-footed, type has been used mostly in West Norway and looks as if a triangle (*fok*) extension had been added to the former type of squaresail. In appearance it is not unlike a lateen sail with the top cut off (Pl. IV p. 49). The bottom of this sail covers the boat all the way from the stem to the deck-house, almost four-fifths of the length of the boat. For that reason the mast has to be further back in the ship with this sail than with the other type. This is the sail which has the *Svipte*, a device for shortening sail which will be explained below (p. 44). The first type has no *Svipte* and there are several reasons for that. According to the saga, then, we have to recognize that Bjarne had the long type of squaresail, and this seems not at all unlikely, since he traded in Western Norway.

It is even likely that the Gokstad ship had the same type of sail, since the mast is stepped so far aft. There has been a great deal of surmising about the place of the mast on the Gokstad ship, but, as far as I know, nobody has been able to give any reason or explanation for its position. But for the type of sail we used in Western Norway the place of the mast on the Gokstad ship would be correct. With such a sail Magnus Andersen would not need the jib (fok) he carried on the *Viking*, which was a copy of the Gokstad ship.

With the right kind of sail, it is very likely that the *Viking* would have made even greater speed than the 11 knots measured by Magnus Andersen. At that speed the jib (fok) was not even used, and one would thus suppose that the sail was stepped too far aft to permit perfect balance.

From various sources we know that in the Viking age it was customary for navigators to observe the height of the sun above the horizon, and in accordance with the observations they determined how far north or south they were from known places, such as the coasts of southern and northern Iceland, or from Bergen or Trondheim in Norway. Similarly we can assume that they knew the positions of the sun with respect to the Shetland and Faeroe Islands. That means that they knew the latitudes of those known places. In navigating across the seas the old Norsemen sought to come in line with those latitudes. And that is, of course, the very same method used by sailing ships right down to our time — with the difference that we have so much better means and instruments to use for the necessary calculations than the Vikings had. The old Norsemen were used to sailing along such latitudinal courses, because most of their traveling over the high seas was in the east-west direction, e.g., from Norway to England, the Shetlands, the Faeroes, Iceland and Greenland.

When the latitude of the destination was known, it was a relatively simple matter to do the navigation, provided the weather permitted them to see the sun, the moon, and the stars. When, however, they met with cloudy and murky weather, difficulties arose. Then they had to find, if possible, the direction of the wind, and sail accordingly, which is fairly possible for an experienced seaman. The

16

different directions of the winds are usually accompanied by special types of weather conditions. There is a difference between the types of weather in connection with winds from the southwest and winds from the north. The seamen of former times learned to distinguish between those types of weather. They also knew and made use of other indications of latitudinal position, such as the presence of whales, different kinds of birds, etc.

The unit of time: the *doegr*.

The Norse voyagers had no conception of hours and minutes. When interpreting the records we have to rely on their unit of time, the *doegr*. There has been some controversy as to whether the *doegr* represents a twelve-hour or a twenty-four-hour period. The answer is surely that a *doegr*'s sailing in coastal waters excluded the hours of darkness but in open waters covered the night as well, since there was no reason to stop. In the sagas, then, the *doegr* usually represents roughly, but only roughly, 24 hours. There must, of course, be an elasticity in the interpretation of times given in the sagas, and this can be illustrated by reference to old records.

In an account of King Harold Hardraade's military expedition to England in A. D. 1066, we find the following:

'So it is said that as the king [with his ships] was located in Solund [outer Sogn] a ship from Greenland arrived there. The leader on that ship was the man called Lika-Lodin. . .

'They put their light boat on the water and rowed over to the king's ship. As Lodin exchanged greetings with the king, the monarch asked him how long they had been at sea. Lodin answered, "7 nights".'

This means that Lodin had taken 7 *doegr* to make the passage from Greenland to Norway, a distance of about 1,600 miles. Seven *doegr,* taking a *doegr* as 24 hours, is 168 hours. But it can be fairly assumed that Lodin set sail from Greenland early in the morning, spent seven nights at sea, and he may well have reported on board the King's ship on his arrival late in the afternoon. If he sailed from

Greenland at 6 a.m. on a Monday morning and reported to the King at 6 p.m. on the following Monday, the voyage would have taken 180 hours.

They recorded their times quite simply according to the passing of a night. There were no references to *long* periods in terms of *doegr*. The number of nights spent during the short successful voyages were easily recalled; but the failures, the long sunless days when they could only ponder their position from dubious signs from, say, the seabirds they saw, or the fish in the waters in which they found themselves, are mentioned in terms of 'many *doegr*', or even of seasons. There is a record in Eirik Raude's saga, for example, of how Thorstein Eiriksson set out on a voyage to Vineland to bring home the body of his dead brother Thorvald. They lost their way and wandered over the ocean throughout the summer and fall, arriving in Lyse-fjord, E. Greenland, at the end of the first week of winter.

The time taken for short passages was often recorded in *doegr*. But it must be remembered that a *doegr* can be based on the passing of a night and thus can represent many more or fewer hours than 24. The term *doegr* will be used freely below.

Bjarne's Voyage

From the *Flateyarbok* we read:

'Learned men tell us that the same summer that Eirik the
Red went to colonize Greenland, twenty-five ships set sail
from Breidafjord and Borgafjord, but only fourteen arrived
at their destination. This was fifteen winters before Christianity was legally established in Iceland [985].

'[Herjulf] had a wife named Thorgerd and their son was
Bjarni, a very promising man. He had taken to foreign
voyages from his youth. This brought him both wealth and
respect, and he used to spend his winters alternately abroad
and with his parents. Bjarni soon had a trading ship of his
own and the last winter that he was in Norway was when
Herjulf undertook the voyage to Greenland with Eirik, and
removed his home there. Herjulf settled at Herjulfsness.

'Bjarni arrived in his ship at Eyrar [in Iceland] in the summer of the same year, in the spring of which his father had
sailed away. Bjarni was much concerned at the news, and
would not discharge his cargo. When his crew asked him
what he meant to do, he replied that he meant to keep to
his custom of passing the winter with his parents; "I will",
said he, "take my ship on to Greenland, if you will accompany me". They all said that they would abide by his decision; upon which Bjarni remarked. "Our voyage will be
considered rash, since none of us have been in Greenland
waters". Notwithstanding this they put to sea as soon as
they were ready, and they sailed for three days before they
lost sight of land; but when the fair wind ceased, and north
winds and fog came on, they did not know where they were
going. This went on for many *doegr*.

'After this period they saw the sun, and so were able to
get their bearings, whereupon they hoisted their sails, and

after sailing that day they saw land, and they discussed among themselves what land this could be; Bjarni said he fancied that it could not be Greenland. They asked him whether he would sail to this land or not. "I am for sailing in close to the land", he said, and when they had done so, they soon saw that the land was not mountainous, and was covered with woods, and that there were small knolls on it, whereupon they left the land on the port side, and let the sheet turn toward it.

'Then, after sailing two *doegr*, they saw another land. They asked Bjarni if he thought this was Greenland; he said that he did not think this was Greenland any more than the first place, for it is said that there are very large glaciers in Greenland. They soon neared this land, and saw that it was a flat country and covered with forest. At this point the fair wind dropped, and the crew suggested that they should land there, but Bjarni would not. They felt that they were short both of wood and water. "You are in no want of either", Bjarni said, and got some abuse from his crew for this remark. He ordered them to hoist sail; they did so, and turned the bows from the land, and sailed out to sea for three *doegr* before a southwesterly breeze; then they saw the third land.

'This land was high and mountainous, with ice upon it. So they asked if Bjarni would put in there, but he refused, since, as he put it, this land appeared to him to be good for nothing. Then without lowering sail they kept on their course along the coast, and saw that it was an island; once more they turned the bows away from land, and held out to sea with the same breeze, but the wind increased, so that Bjarni told them to svipt [see pp. 44f.], and not crowd more sail than their ship and rigging could stand. They now sailed for four *doegr* when they saw the fourth land.

'The crew asked Bjarni if he thought this was Greenland. Bjarni replied, "This is most like what was told me of Greenland, and here we will keep our course towards the land". So they did, and that evening they came to land under a cape, which had a boat on it, and there on that cape lived Herjulf, Bjarni's father, and it is from him that the cape received its name, and has since been called Herjulfsness.'

Bjarne's discovery of America

Bjarne, a young merchant, master of his own ship that was now laden with cargo, was unprepared for the bitter disappointment that he was to face as he sailed proudly into Eyrar. His father Herjulf had had no means, of course, of letting his son know that he had decided to join Eirik the Red's expedition to Greenland, in which over fifty per cent of the 25 vessels were lost.

The reference in the saga to his concern is of interest because of its authentic touch, but the record of his decision not to unload his cargo and of his determination to set out for Greenland immediately is of great importance in view of subsequent events, as will be seen.

His crew had confidence in him, and declared their willingness to attempt the passage. They replenished the ship with water and provisions, no doubt, and set sail. Bjarne's misgivings reflect the hazards of sailing those gloomy unknown seas without navigational instruments, but he was not to be deterred from his purpose — to carry his cargo to the Greenland settlement as swiftly as possible.

Now, with a clear idea of the man and his intentions, of his ship and its capabilities, let us attempt to follow his enforced discovery of the continent of America, with the saga as our guide.

Bjarne and his men had sailed for three *doegr* before they lost sight of Iceland. This indicates that they sailed northward along the coast from Eyrar, where Bjarne landed on coming from Norway, to Cape North, the most northwesterly promontory in Iceland. From there the distance to Greenland is the shortest. This was not only the most natural and safe route to follow, but also the only course known at that time, because it was the one Eirik the Red took, and none but Eirik and his crew had at that time been as far west as western Greenland. At that time the Icelanders knew only what Eirik and his men had told them about the route to Greenland, as well as about the conditions of weather and ice along the east coast of Greenland — as they had learned it during their enforced sojourn of three years in West Greenland. Without maps or instruments it is inconceivable that an experienced seaman like Bjarne would hazard his valuable ship and cargo in an attempt to sail direct from

Reykjanes to Cape Farewell, even if he had known it was the shortest route to Greenland.[5] If they had set such a course from Reykjanes they would not have had to spend three *doegr* at sea before coming far enough out to lose sight of land. Only a few hours would be necessary to sail that distance. On the other hand, three *doegr* in light winds might well have been required if they followed the route of Eirik the Red and lost sight of the coast of Iceland northwest of Cape North.

I have myself sailed along this route to Greenland, and have seen how the Icelandic mountains disappear slowly below the horizon and, shortly thereafter, how the mountain peaks of Greenland arise gradually in the far distance over the ocean. I have also sailed southward along the eastern coast of Greenland from Blosseville to the Lindenowfjord. The most conspicuous landmark along this route is the very high mountain on the coast of Greenland, directly north-west of Iceland. The old Norsemen called it *Kvitserk* (White Gown). The mountain is 12,000 feet high and was the most obvious sailing mark to use in the old sailing directions. In addition one finds icebergs drifting in the ocean near Greenland — a circumstance not encountered in the seas farther south. A third point of interest is the fact that large sections of Greenland's east coast are covered with snow and ice. At certain places high snow-covered mountains rise up into the sky; and here and there stretches of bare and desolate land are seen down by the ocean, while other large sections of this coast are completely covered by the Greenland ice. It is quite obvious that the conditions existing along that route were described to Bjarne in Iceland. But Bjarne could not sail sufficiently far west to see Greenland, because when the mountains in Iceland had disappeared below the horizon, the favorable wind ceased.

The saga describes how the weather became more placid

[5] *Norges Svalbard- og Ishavs-Undersökelser,* Meddelelser nr. 56. Cf. J. Kr. Tornöe, *Lysstreif over Noregsveldets Historie,* pp. 8-14.

and quiet and then thick with fog that came rolling onward, covering the sea. These are common weather conditions in the Greenland Sea: first a calm, then fog, and then a light variable breeze, the *Norrænur* of the saga. The term is not used for a strong northerly wind. *Norrone* and *Vestrone* are the present-day expressions for light breezes, e.g. sunset winds.

When the mists enveloped the ship, Bjarne had altered course to westward so that he could sail over to the east coast of Greenland. The wind was favorable for him then ('north winds ... came on'), but with no sight of the sun and no compass he would have been unable to detect a gradual change. And so it probably came about that the wind backed westward and Bjarne's ship sailed on and on, not westward with a north wind, as he thought, but ever southward with a westerly wind. So many days passed without a sight of the sun that the saga offers no number of *doegr*.

At long last the weather cleared and it became necessary for Bjarne to reach a decision regarding the direction in which he should sail. The saga mentions no direction, but since the land they sighted after one *doegr* of sailing was the coast of America, it is clear that Bjarne's choice was westward. This can be significant; when he had last known his whereabouts he had been off the northwest coast of Iceland with Greenland to the west. He may well have suspected that he had been sailing in circles during those sunless days, and that Greenland was still to be found to the westward.

After one *doegr* on a westerly course they sighted land. Sailing nearer, they perceived that the land was not mountainous, but dotted with knolls. There were many trees.

Bjarne had, of course, no means of knowing where he was. But he could form some idea of the latitude from the height of the sun, say at noon, and thus conclude that they were far off to the south of Greenland's location. In addition the verdure of the forest-covered land also indicated that they were a long way south of their destination. As we have seen, Bjarne had obtained some sort of a description

23

of Greenland before he left Iceland. Thus he knew that Greenland was fairly well covered with ice and snow, and was located far to the north. From personal experience in his travels he knew that the lands located toward the south were the warmest and most verdant and those to the north the coldest and most bleak.

As we have seen, Bjarne's urgent purpose was to reach Greenland, somewhere to the north; he wished to sail his ship there as soon as possible, and the young colony needed his cargo.

As will be seen later, evidence exists that Bjarne and his men were off the coast of Nova Scotia,[6] at a point where the coastline runs in an east northeasterly direction. Now he could sail to the east northeast, keeping his ship at a safe distance from the coast to avoid possible dangerous rocks and shallows, awaiting his opportunity to make a northing, always attempting to edge toward latitudes where physical features ashore and the sun would tell him that he was nearer to conditions which he knew obtained in Greenland.

After clearing Scatari, Bjarne might have decided to alter course in a more northerly direction as soon as he judged it

[6] Several writers have suggested that Bjarne's first land was Cape Cod, but that cannot be correct for several reasons. For one thing Bjarne's description of his third land indicates Baffin Land. This is confirmed by Leiv Eiriksson, see p. 52, and Thorfinn Karlsefne's report (p. 91) from the same land. But according to Bjarne's report he sailed for five *doegr* from his first land to his third land. The distance from Cape Cod to Baffin Land is roughly 1,680 miles. This distance covered in 5 *doegr* gives an average speed of 14 knots, which is too much for a Viking ship. Therefore Bjarne's first land cannot have been Cape Cod, but it could have been Nova Scotia.

On the other hand, A. W. Brögger (*Vinlandsferdene,* p. 74) suggests that Bjarne at first approached the coast of Labrador — but then Bjarne would only have discovered two lands, Markland and Helluland. Bjarne's first land is Leiv's and Karlsefne's third land, where they settled and found grapes, naming it Vineland. Thus Bjarne's first land must have been south of the Gulf of St. Lawrence; this points to Nova Scotia.

24

to be safe. He would soon sight land again — this time seeing Newfoundland for the first time — and be compelled to resume a more easterly course, content to keep well away from the coast without making any attempt to approach it. He would be able to deduce that he had sailed not only too far south, but too far west, and that his chance to alter course to the north would surely come when the land on the northern horizon came to an end.

This opportunity came after they had passed Cape Race. Once again Bjarne was able to steer a northerly course, and this time the hours sped by without the unwelcome appearance of more land to the north forcing him eastward again. Some two *doegr* after leaving the first land they would have been confidently following a coastline with a favorable direction, so well defined that they sailed close enough up to discern glaciers plainly visible on the highlands.

The reference in the saga to the fact that they saw 'another land' implies a passage over a stretch of water with no land in sight. After losing sight of Scatari and altering course more to the north, they would surely have raised Newfoundland in a few hours, during what was in fact a passage over the Cabot Strait. When I read the old records for the first time, I, like most other students of the sagas and writings about this strange voyage, thought that Bjarne had sailed up to the coast as soon as he sighted Newfoundland. But closer study convinced me that this could hardly have happened. The land was of no interest to him. He knew it was not his destination and saw it merely as an obstacle preventing him from taking full advantage of the favorable wind that could carry him to his goal.

One point that seems clear is that Bjarne did not persist with his attempt to sail northward after he had altered course when he considered it safe with Scatari disappearing on his port quarter.

His awareness of land to the westward, and the appearance, after a few hours, of land to the northeast would be enough to persuade him to resume an easterly course.

25

He could not risk the delay involved by sailing into a cul-de-sac; and he clearly sensed that he must sail east of all land so that he could retain the opportunity to sail east to Europe if he should fail to find Greenland.

If pure chance had led him northward through the Strait of Belle Isle he could hardly have omitted to record this important fact. He would have to refer to Newfoundland as an island.

There is no such mention in the saga. Later, moreover, Bjarne was to sail past the northern end of the Strait of Belle Isle and mistake it for a fjord. It will be seen that Leiv and Karlsefne, probably guided by Bjarne's report, did the same, and also sailed east of Newfoundland. All three believed that Labrador and Newfoundland were one land (Markland) with a continuous coastline. According to the Icelandic Annals, Adalbrand and Thorvald were the first explorers to discover that Newfoundland was an island, and were probably the first to sail through the Strait of Belle Isle (1285).

The time given, two *doegr*, can be interpreted as referring to the period during which they sailed continuously, crossing a stretch of sea, and on until they deemed it safe to sail closer to the new land, on which, toward the end of the period, they spotted glaciers in the highlands.

The expression 'they saw land' in this and other sagas must be interpreted with caution. It cannot always have referred to a sudden sight of land after a period with no coast in sight. Nowadays, with accurate instruments and charts available, the navigator sails directly from one point to another. The Norsemen had no such aids. A coastline was to them a lifeline, especially on probing voyages along the American littoral. While keeping at a cautious distance, they were probably seldom out of sight of a coast where they could take shelter on the approach of old enemies such as fog or storms.

Bjarne and his crew had just endured many days of blind sailing, and it does not seem likely that he would have driven his ship back into the uncharted seas. It is possible, of course, that he turned immediately from the coast of Nova Scotia, doubled back in his tracks for one *doegr,* and then made another cast, this time to the northwest. With a strong southwest wind this maneuver could have brought him in to the northern part of Newfoundland about two *doegr* after losing sight of Scatari. This would be in accordance with a strict interpretation of the words of the saga, 'Then, after sailing two *doegr,* they saw another land'. But although, considering that he had not then sighted Newfoundland, but had deduced that he had come too far south and too far west, Bjarne might have contemplated such an attempt, it seems more likely that soon after he had lost Scatari he would try to make a northing and that the two *doegr* mentioned in the saga refers to a period of continuous sailing before approaching *close* to another land.

A point of interest here is the direction of the wind at this stage of the voyage. The saga records that 'they left the land on the port side and let the sheet turn toward it'. Thus if the course of Bjarne's ship was parallel to the coastline the wind during these two days was not blowing from the north or east. Some two *doegr* later, according to the saga, the wind was southwesterly, and Bjarne had covered many miles. It seems reasonable to suppose that he sailed from the first land on the edge of one of the troughs of low pressure that generally move northeastward in these parts, taking advantage of a good breeze from a southerly quarter, probably the southwest.

When Bjarne had sailed for two *doegr,* he says he left his second land before a southwesterly wind. After three more days of sailing, he left his third land before the same southwesterly wind. These statements ring true. Only this southwesterly wind could have enabled Bjarne to sail from Nova Scotia to Baffin Land in five *doegr.* It may well be that there was field ice along Bjarne's route, but the southwesterly wind could have pressed the ice eastward from the land thus clearing the water for Bjarne's passage, all the way to Baffin Land. It is very important to understand the direction of the wind when Bjarne left his first land, a factor not hitherto taken into consideration. After *two and five days'* sailing, Bjarne himself indicates the direction of the wind, and we can see that this is very likely in accordance with the general weather conditions. As soon as he had rounded Cape Race, Bjarne was able to take advantage of an offshore wind, with fairly smooth waters and exceptionally good conditions for a speedy journey along the coast of the new lands.

When they approached the second land his men eagerly asked Bjarne if he thought the land was Greenland. Bjarne answered that this land could not be Greenland any more than the first land they saw, 'for it is said that there are very large glaciers in Greenland'. This expression suggests that they had seen some glaciers before they came into the coast, but not so extensive as the glaciers in Greenland. There are no glaciers in Nova Scotia in the summer. But on the north slopes of the mountains of Newfoundland there are snows or glaciers in the summer. It is very likely that Bjarne and his men had seen these glaciers when they passed Newfoundland and that they now approached the south coast of Labrador, west of Belle Isle. There is no place where they could have seen glaciers on this route except the northern part of Newfoundland.

Following the Newfoundland coast on a course west of north he found, after passing Cape Bauld, the northernmost point of Newfoundland, that he was nearing a low wooded coastline. He would have seen the 1,300 ft. mountains on the Labrador coast, west of Chateau Bay, at a distance of about twenty-five miles. It would appear to him that he was now too far off from the Labrador coast. In order not to lose contact with the coast, it would be necessary for him to lay his course a little more westerly. He would also discover Belle Isle, which he would have to pass to the south at a proper distance. The low coast east of Chateau Bay would probably not be visible at the distance from where Bjarne first had to change his course.

A glance at the chart will show us that Bjarne's bearing

would most likely be on Chateau Bay, east of the mountains.[7]

'They soon neared this land.' This means that they had a good strong breeze from the southwest. Coming into the coast 'the fair wind dropped'. This indicates that they came into Chateau Bay where the mountains southwest of the bay sheltered them from the strong southwest wind. The crew wanted to go ashore. This also suggests that they were in the bay. They 'turned the bows from the land'. This too implies that they were in the bay and sailed straight out of it again.

They could, of course, have sailed into the low coast between Chateau Bay and Battle Harbor, but there they would not have had much shelter against the strong southwesterly wind.

When the wind dropped in the lee of the land the crew suggested that it would be sensible to go ashore. But Bjarne was not in favor of this. So with the prow pointing from the land, they sailed before a wind from the southwest for three *doegr*. This brought them to a third land — with high mountains and glaciers. The description given of this third land fits in well with Baffin Land.

In this case we also have to take for granted that when the records say a third land this means that they had passed across a wide expanse of ocean, which Bjarne thought separated the two lands. Actually, however, there was no such open ocean any of the way from the time they sailed away from the bay in which they had halted in the second land until they came, presumably, to Hudson Strait, which separates Baffin Land from Labrador. Apart from providing a convenient lead, the coast offered protection. Threatened by storm or fog, they could seek shelter in some bay or fjord; otherwise they might find themselves drifting about again on the high seas and in danger once more of

[7] Chateau Bay is perhaps also the place where Leiv Eiriksson later landed in a northeast wind and to which he gave the name 'Markland'. Perhaps Leiv had some of Bjarne's men as pilots, who remembered Chateau Bay from the earlier voyage. (See also p. 56)

becoming lost. In a sheltering inlet on the coast they could await favorable wind and weather conditions, when they could again continue their journey. Thus it was advantageous in several respects to preserve some sort of contact with the coast, while avoiding the risks of an unknown shoreline by sailing at a safe distance out at sea.

As they approached the third land, they could see that it was mountainous and had glaciers like those in eastern Greenland. It now seemed that they must be on the right latitude. They did not lower the sail but continued along the coast for a while until they could see that it was an island they had passed. Then they turned the stern toward the land and sailed out over the ocean with the same favorable wind, i.e., from the southwest.

The southwesterly wind, blowing hard, the saga says, at first, suited their purpose exactly. They sailed onward for four *doegr,* after which they saw a fourth land. By coincidence it was the promontory on which Herjulf, the father of Bjarne, had settled, and which accordingly, had been named 'Herjulfsness'.

Several commentators have found it rather peculiar that Bjarne happened to make a landfall exactly where his father's farm was located. They even go so far as to consider the story quite unreliable. However, with further research they would have found that behind Herjulfsness is located a very high mountain that would naturally be the first landmark, visible from about 90 miles, for a navigator sailing in from the west. Bjarne, no doubt, sighted this landmark.

Other questions may arise in connection with the passage between the third and fourth lands. Herjulfsness, on the southernmost coast of Greenland, is not due east of Loksland, but south of east. It is known that Bjarne was capable of navigating on latitude, and it would seem more likely that he would have sighted Greenland at a more northerly point. There is, however, a southerly current on the west side of the Davis Strait which may well have borne him south during the first part of the passage. It is recorded that he had a southwesterly wind at first, and it may be safely assumed that Bjarne allowed for drift. It is far from unlikely that the ship was carried south of east, so that the first landfall was the high mountain behind Herjulfsness.

Again, the discrepancy between the times recorded for the passage from the first to the second land and that for the final passage may at first appear surprising. The distance from Loksland to Herjulfsness is not much greater than that between Scatari and Chateau Bay. Yet the time recorded for the former is four *doegr,* for the latter only two *doegr.* Here we must refer again to the lack of any attempt at detail in the sagas where such records are concerned, and the elasticity that must be observed when interpreting the term *doegr.* Even in the late summer the nights are short in the latitude of Loksland, and Bjarne may well have altered course to the east in the late evening. We know that the wind increased soon after, so that they had to shorten sail, but we do not know how long this hard breeze blew.

When Bjarne reached Greenland and told about three lands in the far west, it is obvious that thereby was meant only that he had sailed across two wide expanses of ocean, which he thought separated those three countries. He thought that those lands were islands, such as Iceland, Ireland, or England. Obviously, he could not know that a whole continent was hidden behind the coastlines along which he sailed.

Bjarne did not give the lands names, nor did he set foot ashore on any of them. At first it seems strange that a man, convinced he had discovered a new land, did not yield to the temptation to go ashore and explore a little. But it must be emphasized again that Bjarne was many miles off his course with a valuable ship and cargo. Further, it seems highly likely that he had favorable winds for his purpose. When he sighted Newfoundland, it was quite obvious that he was still far to the south of the Greenland latitude; therefore he would not waste any time by stepping ashore to take a look at it: that would only mean an unnecessary delay — in the unknown wilderness. He sailed continuously

31

for two *doegr* from the first country until he made the minor stop recorded in the saga of the voyage. It is possible to believe that Bjarne, taking advantage of a stiff south-westerly breeze, sailed from Nova Scotia to southern Labrador in two *doegr*. As has been pointed out (p. 17), this period need not be interpreted as precisely 48 hours, but may fairly be held to refer to a longer time.

Some authors have claimed that he deviated toward the coast as soon as he sighted the second land and that his position was then off the southernmost promontory of Newfoundland. This is surely a misunderstanding of the account. The coast at the point where they put in after two *doegr* sailing is described in the saga as flat and wooded, a description which fits the southeast sections of the coast of Labrador.

Sailing directions, times, and distances, from the Hauksbok

The old directions for sailing to and from Iceland indicate the amount of time necessary for traveling to various places. The distances between the points mentioned can be ascertained from a map, and by dividing the number of miles by the hours (taking a *doegr* as 24 hours) recorded in the sailing directions it is possible to calculate the approximate speed of the ships.

In the *Hauksbok* [8] we read:

'From Stad in Norway it is 7 *doegr* sailing to Horn, on Iceland's east coast; but from Snaefelsnes, in Iceland, it takes 4 *doegr* to sail to Kvarv in Greenland. From Herdla [nr. Bergen] in Norway one is to sail directly westward to reach Kvarv in Greenland; and to do so one is to sail north of

[8] *Hauksbok* is Are Frode's *Islands Landnamebok* and *Kristni Saga* copied by Lagman Hauk Erlendsen and extended to the year 1334, when he died. Are Frode was born in 1068 and died in 1148.

PLATE I. *The Gokstad ship in the Ship Museum, Oslo. Note the keel (see p. 11).*

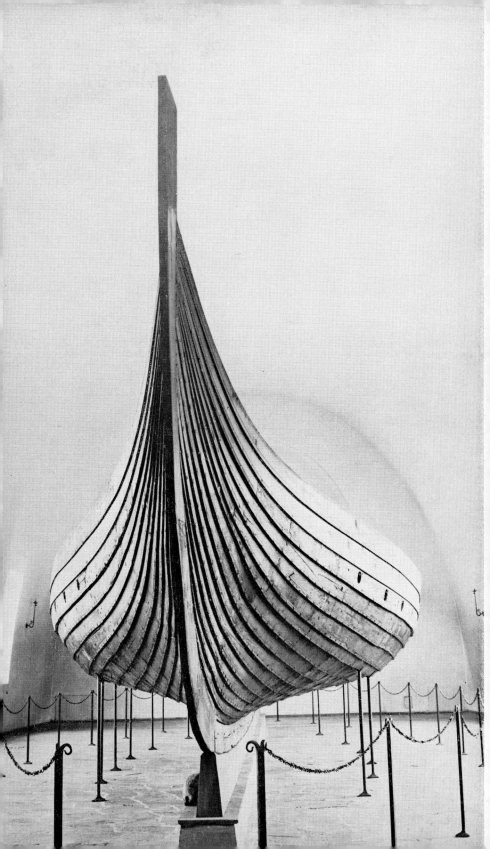

PLATE II. *The fine lines and decorations of the Oseberg ship, in the Ship Museum, Oslo.*

the Shetland Islands, but so far off-shore that one can barely see land in clear weather. Furthermore, one must sail south of the Faeroe Islands, but so far out that only half of the mountains are visible over the horizon. On this course one will also be sailing south of Iceland, but only so far away that one can see the birds and whales common in the Icelandic waters . . .

'From Reykjanes, on Iceland's south coast, it is 3 *doegr* sailing southward to Joeldulaup in Ireland. And from Langanes, on north-eastern Iceland, it is 4 *doegr* on the ocean to Svalbard [Spitsbergen] — north in the "Ocean's Bottom". But it is one *doegr* sailing northward from Kolbeinsey, off Iceland's north coast, to Greenland's deserts [Scoresby Sound].' (See folding map)

Here we are told about two directions from Norway and four from Iceland. The course from Bergen to Greenland is quite correctly indicated; and we are told what means they had of knowing that they were on the right course. The statements about the top half of the mountains in the Faeroe Islands being visible and the birds and the whales in the Icelandic waters may seem rather indefinite, but in the *Landnamebok* it is stated that one must sail twelve miles south of Iceland. To determine so great a distance from ship to land is very difficult indeed. It may thus be much better to follow the rule of birds and whales, as indicated in the *Hauksbok*. Seabirds and whales were obviously to be found mostly on the banks off the coast. Therefore, one was to sail along the outer limits of the fishing banks off southern Iceland.

From the Faeroe Islands to Iceland, along the ocean bed, is located a veritable mountain chain — the so-called Iceland Ridge. Along this ridge a mass of plankton flourishes, on which birds and whales feed. At times the plankton is so plentiful there that the sea is colored red-brown. On both sides of this ridge the water is much deeper and without any of the natural conditions that favor the existence of such plankton. This, in turn, results in the absence of any great number of birds and whales east and west of the ridge. By keeping in contact with the seabirds and whales, one could sail from the Faeroe Islands to Iceland and back again. This was common knowledge among the Vikings, and as I have indicated, they made use of it. Traditional knowledge also covered the other coastal banks and the fishing banks far offshore. With a long line they could measure the depth of the ocean, and by that means find out something about their position; other methods were also at their disposal.

Let us, then, take a look at the length of the courses mentioned in the *Hauksbok*. First let us consider the course mentioned last in the book, i.e., from Kolbeinsey (Mewen Klint) to Greenland's deserts (Scoresby Sound), since it is said to be one *doegr*'s sailing, and may therefore be used as a convenient measurement for the other distances. If one sails northward from Kolbeinsey, as indicated, one will arrive at Scoresby Sound. Kolbeinsey is the natural point of departure for a trip to Scoresby Sound. If one intended to reach Greenland farther west, Cape North would then be the obvious point of departure.

Using a modern chart we find that the distance from Kolbeinsey to Scoresby Sound is about 200 miles. The time for sailing this distance was one *doegr*. Two hundred miles covered in 24 hours gives an average speed of 8.3 knots.

The distance from Langanes in Iceland to Hornsund in Svalbard (Spitsbergen) is about 820 miles, actually four times the distance from Kolbeinsey to Scoresby Sound, indicating the correctness of the saga statement. 820 miles in 96 hours gives an average speed of 8.5 knots.

Then we mark off on the chart the course from Snaefelsness to Cape Farewell (Kvarv), or the Greenland settlement. This route leads from Iceland to a point in the ocean northwest of where the mountain Kvitserk in Greenland can be seen toward the north. From that point they were to sail southwesterly to Angmagssalik and continue along the coast to the settlement in Greenland. The distance is about 790 miles. The sailing time is 96 hours. Thus the average speed is 8.2 knots.

The route from Reykjanes in Iceland to Joeldulaup

(northeastern coast of Ireland), is given three *doegr,* or 72 hours' sailing. The distance of 850 miles in 72 hours gives an average speed of 11.8 knots.

But the length, in *doegr,* of the route from Stad in Norway to Horn (Hornafjörður) in southeast Iceland does not correspond with the length of the other routes. This is because of the generally contrary currents and winds. For all of those distances it is the average time taken that is mentioned; and that average is the result of experience gained in traveling by those routes on several occasions. If the saga had mentioned the course from Horn to Stad, i.e, west-east instead of east-west, it is very likely that it would have taken them only four *doegr,* since the current and the winds would have been favorable most of the time. But seven *doegr* for the Stad-Horn journey seems to correspond with the facts. When Magnus Andersen had sailed his *Viking* for seven *doegr,* in 1893, from Bergen, his longitude corresponded with that of Horn in Iceland. But this amounts to only half the speed attained in sailing the other routes. The average speed is about 8.5 knots.

Some well-known voyages

It is related in the St. Olav saga that Thorarin sailed from Norway to Reykjavik in four *doegr.* That distance is a good deal longer than that from Norway to Horn (Hornafjörður). It is about 900 miles, and the sailing speed would thus be about 9.4 knots. But on this course they had contrary currents; and for that reason one ought to add the distance the current flowed in four *doegr,* in order to find the speed of the ship. However, since the time is mentioned in *doegr* only, we cannot calculate anything about it with exactitude.

The voyage of Lika Lodin has been referred to on page 17. His average speed over the distance from Greenland to Norway of about 1,600 miles must have been over 9 knots.

These passages are not referred to as if they had been achieved at an unusual speed.

Thorarin did not even mention his journey. He merely said that it was '4 nights' from the time he saw King Olav in Norway. We deduce from that statement that he could not have taken any more time crossing the intervening ocean. And Lodin's journey appears to have been quite normal, for nothing more was said about it. It seems reasonable to rely on his statement to the king as being correct, for he was also described as a wise and well-informed person.[9]

For the sake of comparison I shall mention some performances along the coast of Norway by more modern sailing vessels of another type. These concern a type of vessel quite different from the Viking ships. They were constructed for the purpose of carrying heavy cargoes, were shorter, and much deeper and heavier than the vessels of the ancient type. The *yaecht* was not built only for speed but for carrying freight. Rigging and sail, however, were the same as those of the Viking ships. I have seen quite a number of them. *Yaechts* of that kind, carrying goods from Nordfjord to Bergen, gathered quite often in Rugsund, near Hornelen, and lay there awaiting the favorable wind from the north. Skippers of these *yaechts* have claimed that with a good quartering wind they can reach Bergen in 10 hours. The distance is equal to two degrees latitude, or 120 miles. Their speed would thus be 12 knots.

Though we have calculated an average speed of more than nine knots for Lika-Lodin's ship, it is obvious that it often sailed much more rapidly. Since they had no compass, it is reasonable to suppose that they often deviated from the true course; and thus the actual distance sailed may have been considerably longer than the 1,600 miles which we have measured off on the chart. At times the speed must have been a good deal better than the nine knots, but we do not have sufficient information to calculate just what it might have been. We do know, however, that the large open boats, *ottringer* and *femböringer,* which were used by the fishermen in Lofoten right down to our own times,

[9] Tornöe, op. cit., pp. 43-44.

did sail at a speed of 12 knots. The *yaechts* could do the same. Therefore, we have reasons for believing that the Viking ships, constructed especially for speed, could have had a top speed of from 14 to 15 knots, and with favorable winds and currents could have covered long distances at an average speed of 10-12 knots.

In the *Bygdebok*, volume I, page 238, for Buksnes parish in Lofoten, we find the following statement:

'. . . But that summer (1881) Mr. Mathias Salomonsen of Leknes made with his *yaecht* undoubtedly the most rapid journey to Bergen he had ever accomplished. The trip south was made in 79 hours . . . He himself says that it was an unusually rapid trip.'

I mention this case even though the sailing here involves following the customary leads among the skerries and islets along the coast. Clearly, journeys of this kind cannot easily be compared with those across the open ocean. From Buksnes in Lofoten to Bergen it is 8 degrees latitude or about 480 miles in a straight line. However, Salomonsen sailed across the Vestfjord in order to enter the customary and protected leads. These zigzag between the islets and skerries continually; and this makes the actual mileage sailed much more than a straight course. However, even if we add only 60 miles, his *yaecht* still had an average speed of seven knots. On such a vessel the crew was small in number. Usually the skipper was also the pilot; and it was seldom he had on board another competent man to whom he could trust the *yaecht* and cargo within the leads. Thus it was customary to lie at anchor during the darkest part of the nights in order to catch some necessary sleep. If we then subtract the hours of rest from the 79 hours on the trip south, it is apparent that Salomonsen's *yaecht* must have had a speed of 9 to 10 knots, when under sail, in order to reach Bergen in 79 hours.

Now with these facts we can compare the voyage of Bjarne:

from Nova Scotia to southeastern Labrador

                    approx. 600 miles in 2 *doegr*
from Labrador to Loksland (Baffin Land)

                    approx. 700 miles in 3 *doegr*
from Loksland to Greenland

                    approx. 600 miles in 4 *doegr*

                    _____

                    approx. 1,900 miles in 9 *doegr*

The average speed for the distance will thus be 8.8 knots.

A hypothetical reconstruction

At this juncture, with the probability established that Bjarne's three lands were Nova Scotia, Newfoundland with Labrador, and Baffin Land, an attempt at a hypothetical reconstruction of the voyage might be of interest.

The saga relates how Bjarne was driven off his course and lost his bearings. But after many days the weather cleared and a sight of the sun enabled him to determine the various directions.

Before he lost the sun Bjarne was sailing from Iceland to Greenland on a favorable wind, probably from the north. As he sailed on, this direction changed imperceptibly to the west, and for many days the ship sailed southward.

One afternoon the wind freshened and at last they caught sight of the sun on the starboard bow. As they sailed on they saw that it was sinking toward their starboard horizon and so they knew in which direction the west lay.

Bjarne decided that his wisest course would be to make a cast westward. He did not realize yet how fast and how far he had been driven south, and it seemed possible to him that Greenland still lay to the west and that he would soon make a landfall.

The following afternoon they did indeed sight land to westward. But as they drew nearer, Bjarne's hopes fell. Here were no glacier-covered highlands, but a green coast with little hills and woods. No doubt curiosity mingled with his

38

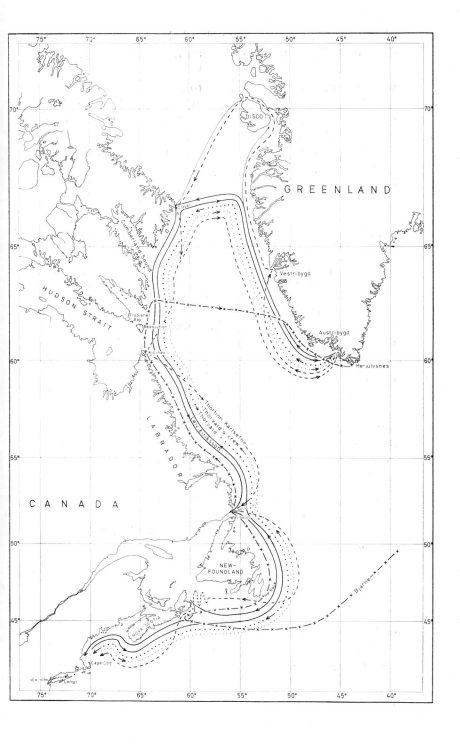

disappointment, but Bjarne decided that he must move on at once. Now he knew that he was too far south, and it would profit him nothing to sail further westward. So they went about, 'let the sheet turn toward' this new land, and sailed away to the east northeast with the land to port. This maneuver indicates that the wind was blowing from a southerly direction.

It has been shown that Bjarne could not have sailed up to the land any further south than Nova Scotia. Let us take his turning point as Cape Canso, and allow him an average speed of 10 knots for the five *doegr* passage from Nova Scotia to Baffin Land.

Bjarne obtained a good view of the physical features of the new land, which indicates that it was daylight when he approached. Let us say that it was late on a Sunday afternoon. Before he put his ship about and sailed away in the evening he would have a good idea of the direction of the coastline. For safety's sake he moved away from it but without losing it entirely as darkness advanced. It is unlikely that the few hours of night were so black that the lookout lost sight of the dark line of coast on the port side.

But at dawn Scatari would be on the port quarter and they were, it seemed, about to lose sight of land. Bjarne's first thought was the possibility of altering course more to the north, but his sailorly wisdom warned him that there might be rocks and shallows continuing from Scatari in a northeasterly direction.

Thus we can imagine him sailing on for a time, and then, with Scatari now out of sight, say at 6 a.m. on Monday morning, ordering a change of course northward.

Now they had a following breeze, and not many hours passed before they saw, to their disappointment, a coastline on the horizon, running straight across their path. This could not be any part of Greenland, as Bjarne well knew. He was much too far south. This could only be a land which he must somehow sail around, and the only safe way to do so was to alter course to the east as soon as possible. Around noon on the Monday, then, the ship was sailing

40

eastward. During the night Bjarne would keep well away from the dark patches, Miquelon Island and then Burin Peninsula, which he would have passed by midnight. In the light of dawn, with one *doegr* gone, they would observe with impatience that there was still a land to the north which must be circumvented. But by noon on Tuesday their hopes were rising again, for they had passed Cape Race, and now, surely, the coastline ran in a more promising direction.

For the second time Bjarne altered course, and with the wind still favorable, they approached Cape Bonavista at midnight.

Before darkness they could see the course for several hours along the coast, and at dusk they could navigate by the North Star. Maybe they had moonlight and could see the coast all the night. With a southwesterly wind the sea would be smooth and they would have the best conditions for good speed. Newfoundland is wooded and fair for farmland. So they understood that they were still far to the south and Bjarne pressed forward as fast as ship and rigging could take him. On Wednesday, at 12 noon, they had added 120 more miles to their journey, and they were sailing off Groais Island.

Bjarne and his men proceeded onward on their course for several more hours, until 6 p.m. on Wednesday. At the same speed they sailed right up to the southeast coast of Labrador, and entered Chateau Bay. By now two *doegr* had elapsed since they departed from their first land, Nova Scotia.

Along such a low and level coast the sea is often shallow. Therefore Bjarne turned his ship about and stood right out from the coast, through the same waters he had just sailed in by, in order to be sure that the ship should not go aground. At a safe distance from the coast, he then altered course to the northeast along the shoreline. At Battle Harbor he could set a course to the north, and at Domino Harbor he would sail west of north, in accordance with the direction of the coastline.

Having sailed away from Chateau Bay at 6 p.m. on Wednesday, they continued for 24 hours along the coast. With a speed of 10 knots we find them at 6 p.m. on Thursday off Cape Harrison. They continued for 24 hours and added 240 more miles to their journey northward. On Friday, at 6 p.m., they were somewhere outside Saglek Bay. From there they sailed for another 24 hours along the coast, past Hudson Strait, and reached up to a third land, which was high and mountainous and covered with glaciers. This clearly indicates Baffin Land. With their average speed of 10 knots they were off Loksland at 6 p.m. on Saturday. Without lowering their sail they continued along the coast and saw what they took to be a promontory as they approached from the south. Soon, however, when they had sailed past this land, they could see that a sound separated it from the mainland, and they knew it was an island. We can be sure that this island could not have been Resolution Island or Edgell Island, as they are situated too far from the mainland.

But there are some islands outside Loksland. One of these is very likely to be the island where Bjarne altered course to the east. An island is mentioned as a sailing mark for Helluland. Northeast of the island of Loksland there are several smaller islands. These eastern islands are the obvious point of departure for a ship sailing over to Greenland because they are located so far to the east of Baffin Land. A large-scale chart is necessary to follow this in detail.

Then they turned the stern of the ship toward the land and sailed out over the ocean — with the same favorable wind (from the southwest). The wind was so strong at first that they had to shorten sail. They continued sailing eastward for four *doegr* and then arrived at the coast of Greenland. They landed at Herjulfsness.

The times recorded for the passages between the four lands must be given a broad interpretation. The elasticity of the term *doegr* has been mentioned above. Allowance can fairly be made for a few hours more or less for the voyage between each land. For example, according to our hypothesis Bjarne sailed away from his first land at 6 a.m.

on a Monday. It is a matter of conjecture whether he reckoned his two *doegr* from the time he altered course or from the time the land disappeared below the horizon. And whether he arrived off the southeast coast of Labrador at 5 a.m. or 6 p.m. on Wednesday he would still describe the time taken as two *doegr*. Precisely how these times are divided between the given distances can never be known. But in any case, it has been shown earlier that the ship was fast enough to cover the distances in the time given in all instances, when we compare it with time spent on voyages between more familiar points; for instance, the distances from Greenland to Norway, Norway to Iceland, Iceland to Ireland, Iceland to Spitsbergen, and also Magnus Andersen's voyage with the *Viking* from Norway to America in 1893.

The saga about Bjarne's voyage.
Fact or fiction?

Did Bjarne see the coasts of Nova Scotia, Newfoundland, Labrador, and Baffin Land — or is the story plain fiction, made up in Iceland about 400 years later?

Such eminent scholars as Torfæus, Gerhard Schöning, Magnússon and Rafn, among others, have always considered the saga about Bjarne's discoveries a true story. This opinion was contested by Professor Gustav Storm in his *Studies on the Vineland Voyages* (1887).[10] Storm rejected the saga account because he worked out the sailing distances reckoning on a *doegr* of 12 hours rather than one of 24 hours. When he could not get the sailing distances to fit in, he rejected the saga as fiction.

Later, Professor Fridtjof Nansen [11] rejected all the Vineland sagas as fairy tales. Many scholars have given credence to Storm's and even Nansen's criticisms, but, as we shall see, these objections are ill-founded.

If the saga of Bjarne's voyage were not authentic and contemporary, but a fictional account produced by a writer

[10] *Aarböger for nordisk Oldkyndighed*, 1887.
[11] *In Northern Mists*, 1911.

43

some 400 years later, as has been suggested, one would expect to find discrepancies. As it is, the facts related in Bjarne's saga dovetail very well. The references to wind and weather, visibility, and conditions ashore, need give no rise to doubting calculations. It has been shown that Bjarne's ship was speedy enough to have covered the distance in the time stated, given favorable winds. His motives for keeping on the move were simple enough.

Some misunderstanding has been caused by the reference to 'svipting', on the eastward passage from the third land to Greenland. Earlier writers seem to have been confused by the expression. Rafn, whose suggestion that Bjarne encountered a storm on leaving Baffin Land [12] seems to be unfounded, says that Bjarne ordered the sail to be lowered. Gathorne-Hardy maintains that he told them to reef. I do not believe that either of these interpretations is correct. *'Svipte'* was neither lowering nor reefing the sail.

When the wind increased so much that they had to reduce the sail, they could do so in two ways. One way was to 'svipt' the sail, and the other was to reef it. *'Svipte'* means to fold vertically five to seven pieces of cloth in the middle of the sail. For that purpose they had a wooden thimble sewn into the seams between the cloths on each of the five seams. Through these thimbles a rope passed horizontally across the sail. Each end of this rope was sewn into the sail. Between the second and the third thimble was a loose thimble on the rope, spliced into the end of a rope hanging down from the sail to the ship. When a man hauled on this rope, he folded more or less the middle of the sail. This was to 'svipt' the sail. These ropes were called *svipte* or *sifte*.[13] I have had personal experience of such sails. When

[12] *Grönlands Historiske Mindesmærker* Vol. III, pp. 885-86.

[13] See Hans Ross, *Norsk Ordbog*, Christiania, 1895: *Svifta* = to pull, hence pull together, or close, a sail. (Eng. brail) Also *syfta* (Sogn); *svifting* m. = hauling lines in a sail. (Eng. brails) Also *syfte* (Ytre Sogn). Old Norse *svipting*.

See also Ivar Aasen's *Norsk Ordbog, med dansk forklaring,* Kristiania 1918, under *Handsyfte.* and Johan Fritzner's *Ordbog over Det gamle norske Sprog,* Kristiania 1896, under *Svipta.*

the wind increased or decreased, a man hauled or slackened the rope. In that way one man could regulate the pressure on ship and rigging and at the same time keep maximum speed. To 'svipt' was the easiest way to reduce sail, but it could not be used under all circumstances; in a storm they always reefed the sail, because too much pressure on the *svipte* could split the sail. 'Svipting' was mostly used with moderate quartering winds because then it was easiest to fold the sail vertically.

The saga says that the wind earlier on was from the southwest, and even if it had changed over to west or northwest it would still be appropriate to 'svipt' the sail on the course from Baffin Land to Greenland. If the saga had told, for example, that they 'svipted' the sail in a storm or in a headwind — then we could suspect fiction. But the description, 'the same breeze, but the wind increased', indicates typical conditions for 'svipting'. There is no disagreement in the saga in the matter of the weather, the visibility, the wind, the course of the ship and the sailing. The narrative about Bjarne's voyage is very unlikely to be fiction.

On the other hand, bearing in mind the fact that none of the Vineland expeditions could set course for Greenland before they came to Baffin Land, we can see that Bjarne never could have reached as far south as Cape Cod, as Holand and Pohl surmise. Even though his ship has been shown to be speedier than generally supposed, Bjarne could not possibly have been farther south than the neighborhood of Halifax.

These two authors also speak of Bjarne's course to the northeast, but the saga never gives a hint regarding Bjarne's course. The only way to find Bjarne's course is to have in mind that, for several reasons, he had to see the coast and at the same time be at a safe distance from it. These two authors also suggest that Bjarne sailed west of Newfoundland; but for a number of reasons this cannot be true. Bjarne had always to sail east of the land in order to reserve the opportunity to sail east to Europe, if he could not find

Greenland. The island Bjarne mentions is not Newfoundland, which he would have had to call a land, but it could be the island outside Loksland on the coast of Baffin Land.[14]

Doubts of the truth of the saga engendered by the allegation that Bjarne was in too much of a hurry to set foot ashore can be reasonably dispelled. As stated above, Bjarne did not unload his ship in Iceland but took the commodities, brought from Norway, along to Greenland. This may have been a compelling reason for not wishing to land in America: he wanted to bring the valuable cargo to Greenland as soon as possible. The cargo and ship may have represented all he possessed; and obviously the pioneer settlers in Greenland could make use of all his wares. His cargo would thus be of great benefit to the settlers and quite profitable to Bjarne. In any case, it is always considered a risky proceeding to sail close up to an unknown shore with a laden ship. It seems very plain, therefore, why Bjarne was so reluctant to land in America, and why he was so anxious to utilize the favorable winds to reach his point of destination as soon as possible. If he was delayed in this endeavor, he might be overtaken by the dreaded winter storms during the approaching fall.

Bjarne understood that the settlers on Greenland were busy building their first houses for the winter; probably Bjarne and his men would have to do the same, as it was the first year anyone had settled in Greenland. They also had to provide food for themselves for the winter, so it is no wonder that Bjarne was in a hurry and would brook no delay in America.

Aftermath

It is obvious that, as soon as Bjarne arrived in the settled part of Greenland, his discoveries of new lands in the west

[14] Hjalmar R. Holand, *Explorations in America before Columbus,* 1956, pp. 29-31; Frederick J. Pohl, *The Lost Discovery,* pp. 21-35.

would become known. He necessarily had to travel about among the settlers to vend his wares and this would automatically result in the spreading of the news regarding his involuntary exploits. Awareness of the undoubted existence of new lands obviously seeped into Europe through the conversations of merchants and other travelers. Furthermore, Bjarne himself went over the sea to Earl Eirik in Norway, where he told about his experiences and the new lands. He also became a member of Earl Eirik's bodyguard, in which group, it is related in the sagas, they conversed a great deal about his discoveries and blamed him to some extent for not landing anywhere. The well-known historian Gerhard Schöning concluded that this discussion took place in the years 988-989. At that time Earl Eirik ruled Vemork in Norway, in conjunction with the Danish king.[15] The following summer Bjarne returned to Greenland, where the pioneering settlers discussed and debated the possibilities of an expedition westward to find those new lands again.

For a private person it was naturally a difficult undertaking to try to found a new colony in an unknown land. Usually it was necessary for a king and a government to sponsor and assist such an enterprise. And it is quite possible that Bjarne undertook the voyage to Norway (988-989) in order to arouse Earl Eirik's interest in the new lands. However, Earl Eirik does not seem to have become enthusiastic; but this may have been due to the political conditions in Norway at the time.

The settlement in West Greenland, from which any such further attempt to establish a new colony had to proceed, was obviously small and of little account. *We must remember that Bjarne and his men found the new lands in the same year, 986, in which the colony in Greenland was founded.* It was also, of course, necessary to build homes and create life-sustaining conditions in Greenland before the adventurers could undertake another colonizing enterprise westward to America.

[15] Most scholars forget this, and so date Bjarne's journey after the year 1000, when Earl Eirik ruled western Norway.

47

However, fifteen years later the Greenland colony had become so extensive and prosperous that Leiv, the son of Eirik the Red, was able to organize and equip a colonizing expedition to the new lands. Perhaps the main factor that made this possible was the fact that the period of civil wars in Norway had come to an end.

Model of a sixth century Viking ship, in the Ship Museum, Bergen. This was a fairly small vessel. Note the rudder, and the ship's clean lines.

The Indian arrow head from Greenland which may be the one that killed Thorvald (see p. 82 n.).

PLATE III

PLATE IV.

a) *The older type of squaresail from North Norway. See p. 15.*

b) *The long-footed squaresail from West Norway. Note the thimbles and ropes for 'svipting' the sail (cf. p. 44).*

Leiv's Discovery of Vineland

We read from the *Flateyarbok:*

'There was now much talk of exploration. Leiv, Eirik the Red's son from Brattahlid, went to Bjarni Herjulfsson and bought a ship from him, and engaged a crew of thirty-five men. Leiv asked his father Eirik still to be leader of the exploration.

'Now they prepared their ship, and when they were ready they put out to sea, and they found first the country which Bjarni found last. There they sailed up to the land, and having cast anchor and lowered a boat went ashore, and saw no grass there. The background was all great glaciers, and all the intermediate land from the sea to the glaciers was like one flat rock, and the country seemed to them destitute of value. Then Leiv said, "We have not failed to land, like Bjarni; now I will give this country a name, and call it Helluland [the land of the flat stone]". Thereupon they returned on board ship, after which they sailed to sea and discovered the second land. Again they sailed up to the land and cast anchor, then lowered the boat and went ashore.

'This land was low-lying and wooded, and wherever they went there were wide stretches of white sand, and the slope from the sea was not abrupt. Then Leiv said, "This land shall be given a name from its resources, and shall be called Markland [wooded-land]", after which they returned to the ship as quickly as possible. And they sailed after that in the open sea with a northeast wind, and were out two *doegr* before they saw land, toward which they sailed, and coming to an island which lay to the north of the mainland, they landed on it, the weather being fine, and looked around; and they perceived that there was a dew on the grass, and it came about that they put their hands in the dew, and carried it to their mouths, and thought that they never had known anything so sweet as that was. Then they went back to the ship, and sailing into the sound which lay between the island and the cape which ran north from the mainland, they steered a westerly course past the cape. It was very shallow there at low tide, so that their ship ran aground, and soon it was a long way from the ship to the sea. But they were so very eager to get to land that they would not wait for the tide to rise under their ship, but instead hurried ashore where a river came out of a lake; but when the sea had risen under their ship they took the boat and rowed to the ship, and took her up to the river and afterward into the lake, where they cast anchor, and carrying their leather kitbags ashore they put up shelters, but later, on deciding to pass the winter there, they made large houses.

'There was no want of salmon, either in the river or in the lake, and bigger salmon than they had seen before; the amenities of the country were such, as it seemed to them, that no cattle would need fodder there in the winter; there came no frost in the winter, and the grass did not wither there much. Day and night were more equally divided there than in Greenland or Iceland: on the shortest day the sun was up over the Icelandic marks for both supper and breakfast time. ['eykt-place and dagmal-place on the shortest day of the year']

'It happened one evening that a man of their party was missing, and this was Tyrker the southerner. Leiv was much distressed by this, for Tyrker had been long with his father and him, and had been very fond of Leiv as a child: so now Leiv, after finding great fault with his men, prepared to look for him, taking a dozen men with him. But when they had gone a little way from the camp Tyrker came towards them, and was received with joy. Leiv saw at once that his fosterfather was in good spirits . . .

'Tyrker had a projecting forehead and a very small face with roving eyes; he was a small and insignificant man, but handy at every kind of odd job.

'Then Leiv said to him; "Why are you so late, my fosterfather, and why did you separate from your companions?" Tyrker at this spoke for a long time in Turkish, rolling his eyes and grimacing, but the others did not distinguish what he was saying. But a little later he said in Norse, "I did not

50

go much further than you, but I have found something fresh to report. I found vines and grapes". "Is that true, fosterfather?" said Leiv. "Certainly it is true", he replied, "for I was born where there was no lack of vines or grapes."

'Now they slept that night, but in the morning Leiv said to his crew, "We will now do two things, keeping separate days for each; we will gather grapes and cut down vines, and fell wood, to make a cargo for my ship"; and this suggestion was adopted. The story goes that their pinnace [afterboat] was full of grapes. So a cargo was cut for the ship, and in spring they made ready and they sailed away, and Leiv gave the land a name according to its resources, and called it Vineland . . .

'So after this they put to sea, and the breeze was fair till they sighted Greenland, and the mountains under the glaciers. Then a man spoke up and said to Leiv: "Why are you steering the ship so much into the wind?" "I am paying attention to my steering", replied Leiv, "but to something else as well: what do you see that is strange?" They said they could see nothing remarkable. "I do not know", said Leiv "whether it is a ship or a reef that I see". Then they saw it and said that it was a reef. But Leiv was longer sighted than they, so that he saw men on the reef. "Now", said Leiv, "I wish that we should beat up-wind, so as to reach them if they need our help and it is necessary to assist them, and if they are not peaceably disposed we are masters of the situation and they are not". So they came up to the reef, and lowered their sail and cast anchor: and they launched a second dinghy they had with them.

'Then Tyrker asked who was the captain [of the ship-wrecked party]. "His name is Thori", was the reply, "and he is a Norseman, but what is your name?" Leiv told his name. "Are you a son of Eirik the Red of Brattahlid?" said Thori. Leiv assented. "Now", said Leiv, "I will take you all on board my ship, and as much of your stuff as the ship can hold." They agreed to these terms, and afterward they sailed to Eiriksfjord with this freight, until they came to Brattahlid where they unloaded the ship. After that Leiv invited Thori and Gudrid his wife, and three other men to stay with him, and procured lodgings for the rest of the crews, both Thori's men and his own. Leiv took fifteen men from the reef; he was called Leiv the Lucky, from then on. So Leiv gained both wealth and honor.

Comment on Leiv Eiriksson's
expedition to Vineland

There is every indication that Leiv sailed from his home at Brattahlid (Julianehaab), Greenland, and followed Bjarne's route in reverse. It is hardly possible to justify the belief of Pohl[16] and Holand[17] that Leiv sailed from Brattahlid to Newfoundland without chart or compass, a distance of 700 miles. Even if he had known the direction of Newfoundland, an experienced seaman like Leiv would not have risked the head-winds and caprices of the North Atlantic over such a distance, especially when he knew of a safer way.

I may be reminded that Leiv had sailed from Greenland to Norway, which was even further away than Newfoundland. But there is a big difference between these two voyages. To Norway Leiv sailed on the latitude, due east all the way. To sail to Newfoundland, he would have to take a longitudinal observation and for that he would need a chronometer, but at that time there were no such things. For that reason it was much harder, at least in daylight, to sail north or south than east or west. In the daytime they steered by the sun and tried to keep due east; and at night they could steer only by the North Star. They sailed till they sighted land and so they did not need to take longitudinal observations. Leiv knew how much simpler it was to sail to Baffin Land than Newfoundland and we can be sure that he took the easier way.

Further evidence against Newfoundland and in favor of Baffin Land is Leiv's description of Helluland, where, he says, there was no grass. This indicates Baffin Land. Newfoundland, however, is farmland with plenty of grass and woods. Here there are no great ice-covered mountains in the summer time, but the ice and the mountains described by Leiv *are* found in Baffin Land.

As Leiv had no chart and no compass, it was natural for him to try to find the shortest sea-passage from Greenland

16 Op.cit., pp. 45-47.
17 Op.cit., pp. 40-41.

to Baffin Land. The distance from Brattahlid to Resolution Island is about 500 miles. The distance from the western settlement (Godthaab) to Cape St. David (Baffin Land) is 350 miles. From Holstensborg to Cape Dyer it is only 200 miles. It would prove good sense for Leiv to go north along the coast before he crossed over. As we shall see later, Thorfinn Karlsefne sailed all the way north to Disco Island before he set his course for Cape Dyer. How far north Leiv went before he crossed over depends on his knowledge of Baffin Land. It is not outside the bounds of possibility that there had already been some hunting expeditions to Baffin Land. Maybe all later expeditions to Vineland went north to Disco.

Most of those who have written about the Vineland voyages have not understood that Helluland had to be Baffin Land. They have tried to identify Helluland with the coast of Labrador or Newfoundland and have thus pushed Markland and Vineland out of their more obvious locations — distorting the whole account in this saga.

South of Hudson Strait grassland abounds. Labrador is forested as far north as Hamilton Inlet. Newfoundland is farmland, and bears no resemblance to Helluland as described in the sagas. Newfoundland is situated more than 10 degrees of latitude south of Greenland and south of Baffin Land. Greenland and Baffin Land are on the same latitude and the natural conditions are much alike.

Bjarne neither landed on nor named his third land. Leiv, however, went ashore, looked around him, and found that Helluland was a fitting name for it. It may well be that they landed somewhere north of the island off Loksland, or in Frobisher Bay. Following the coast they would see Edgell Island and Resolution Island before passing over Hudson Strait to Labrador, Bjarne's second land. They had to sail Bjarne's route in reverse along the coast because there was no other route to take before they came to the Strait of Belle Isle. There they saw the woods on the land, as Bjarne had told them, and they had Belle Isle as a sailing mark.

Again they sailed close up to the shore, anchored their ship, launched their rowboats, and landed. There were extensive stretches of white sand where they went, and the land along the shore was flat. Then Leiv said: 'This land we must name in accordance with its natural conditions and call it *Markland*', that is, wooded land or land of vegetation. It seems quite clear that that land could not have been any other than the modern Labrador. Furthermore, it seems rather unlikely that they gave this name only to a part of Labrador and another name, such as Vineland, to the remainder of that land, as some writers in this field have contended. It is almost certain that Leiv and his men were unaware of the fact that Newfoundland and Labrador did not constitute an unbroken stretch of land. With Bjarne, perhaps, as their only mentor, they could easily have taken the Strait of Belle Isle to be only a fjord, and Newfoundland thus to be a part of Markland.

So far Leiv had followed Bjarne's route. But when he had sailed as far south as the Strait of Belle Isle, the question could arise as to whether he left Bjarne's route, sailed through the Strait of Belle Isle and continued along the coast of Quebec toward the St. Lawrence River. Some authors have thought so because they have failed to understand what was meant by Bjarne's three countries, and have thereby mistaken his route, which is the key to the understanding of all the Vineland expeditions.

We know that Leiv's goal was to find the southernmost of the three countries, Bjarne's first land — that land which was later given the name of Vineland by Leiv because of the grapevines which grew there. It is certain that the route had been explained to him in Greenland. Why should Leiv then start seeking a different route to Vineland?

They did not know that the Strait of Belle Isle was anything but a fjord. Even if they guessed it was a sound, they did not know where it led to. And this, of course, was in Markland — whereas they were trying to reach Bjarne's first land. Since Bjarne had sailed along the east coast of Newfoundland and thought this belonged to his second land, then, according to this calculation, they were not at the southern point of Markland, but off the coast halfway along this land. Why should they try to find a route westward through Bjarne's second land in order to reach his first land — when they understood, according to Bjarne's account, that the first land was far to the south of where they lay, and that a stretch of ocean intervened between the two lands? It is unlikely that they would start experimenting with the problem of finding a route through Markland when there was no necessity for it; besides, there were no definite indications that this sound, if sound it were, would lead them to Vineland.

There is further evidence that they did not sail through the Strait of Belle Isle. If they had done so and had followed the coast to the St. Lawrence River, they would have found that Markland and Vineland were connected and not two separate lands. That Leiv at the time did not know this is proved by the fact that he, together with his brother, Thorvald, planned the expeditions which were to *sail around* Vineland, which they thought to be an island like England, Ireland, and Iceland. (When Iceland was discovered, there were many who sailed around it, such as Gardar and Gunbjorn.) Thorvald dispatched his boat from Leiv's *Budir* with instructions to try to sail south of Vineland and over to the west coast. Thorvald himself went with the larger ship hoping to sail around Vineland from the north, north of Nova Scotia. This shows that neither of them had entered by the St. Lawrence River, for then they would have discovered that the northern part of Markland, i.e. Labrador and Vineland, was continuous. It was on this voyage that Thorvald was killed by the Indians, before he got north of Nova Scotia. The connection between Markland and Vineland, therefore, was not discovered. They still believed these were two separate pieces of land.

When Leiv left Markland (Labrador) with a northeast wind, he sailed for two *doegr* and reached an island situated to the north of the next land (Vineland). If he had continued along the coast of Quebec to the St. Lawrence River, as some writers have contended, it is obvious that he could not have come to another land, neither could he, along this coast, have come to an island situated 'north of the land'. But Leiv *could* have reached Scatari by sailing through the Strait of Belle Isle, and along the west coast of Newfoundland. But then he would have discovered that Newfoundland was a separate land, to which he would have given a name, and he certainly would have recorded his discovery. From his silence on the point, however, we can take it for granted that Leiv sailed east of Newfoundland, as did Bjarne and Thorfinn Karlsefne. According to the *Flateyarbok*, Thorfinn Karlsefne also sailed to Leiv's *Budir*. When he passed Newfoundland, he had the land on the starboard side; that is, he sailed east of Newfoundland. Leiv Eiriksson recorded a northeast wind when he left the point where he went ashore in Markland. If he had had the same wind earlier along the coast of Labrador, he could probably not have approached the lee-shore to make a landing. But, when he had reached south to about the 52nd parallel he would have found smooth waters for landing in the northeasterly wind, especially in Chateau Bay. The land there is flat and wooded, as both Bjarne and Leiv stated. Farther west, the coast is steeper and more rocky and there is no harbor or shelter against the northeast wind. If an expedition to this coast of Labrador were to take the saga with them as a guide, it is likely that they could locate the place where Leiv landed and which he named Markland.[18] As we have seen, if Leiv did not sail westward through the Strait of Belle Isle, he would have had to leave the coast and sail in the direction of Cape Bauld on Newfoundland.

It is reasonable to assume, then, that they went ashore and took a look at the forest and the landscape and perhaps helped themselves to wood and water before they left the coast of Labrador.

But this stretch along the coast of Newfoundland we have covered earlier in connection with Bjarne's voyage. It is

[18] See also footnote 7, p. 29.

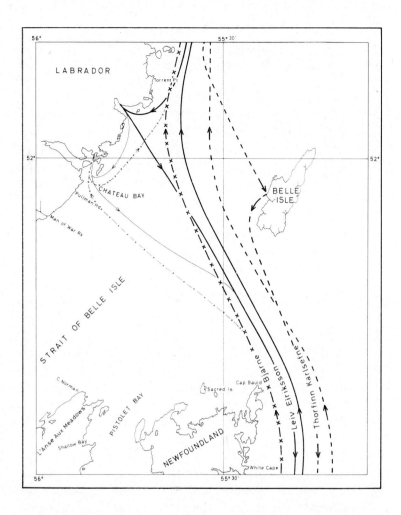

this region of Bjarne's second land at which we found that
he arrived after sailing for two *doegr* from Nova Scotia.

Bjarne's description of this coast agrees with Leiv's. Leiv
says of it: 'This land was low-lying and wooded, and . . .
there were wide stretches of white sand, and the slope from
the sea was not abrupt [*osebratt*].' Both say the same about
the land and the forest, but Bjarne does not mention the
sand and the seashore; and that is understandable since he
did not go ashore.

In his book, *The Vineland Voyages*,[19] John R. Swanton gives a modern description of this coast: 'The official map of Canadian forests (Atlas of Canada, pages 17-18) shows "densely wooded northern forest" between Hamilton Inlet and Sandwich Bay.' H. G. Watkins[20] reports that 'Southern Labrador is so thickly wooded that it is impossible to do any plantable work. Even the high hills are usually covered with trees, and for the most part it is an undulating country with no outstanding peaks.' This, of course, agrees with the accounts of Bjarne and Leiv. Bjarne says that the fair wind diminished when they came nearer to the coast, and it is quite probable that the southwesterly wind on which they sailed became lighter when they neared the shore and the land sheltered them against the wind. Chateau Bay does in fact afford shelter from both southwest and northeast winds. Before Leiv's next halt, he sailed for two *doegr,* assisted by a northeasterly wind.

We quote from the saga about Leiv's journey from this place in Markland:

'And they sailed after that in the open sea with a northeast wind and were out two *doegr* before they saw land, to which they sailed; and coming to an island which lay to the north of the mainland, they landed on it, the weather being fine, and looked around.'

They tasted the dew on the grass and found that it was sweet. This means that they had arrived at Vineland the Good, because in no other place were there such wonderful things. They had, it seems, sailed across the sea from Cape Race on Newfoundland to Nova Scotia. That they saw land after sailing for two *doegr* from Markland and that they sailed into the shore means, undoubtedly, that they came in from the open sea. During the last part of the voyage they cannot have been following a coastline, since it is pointed out that they came to another land. Leiv, then, had followed Bjarne's route from the southern part of the coast

[19] The Smithsonian Institute, Washington. D.C. 1947, p. 49.
[20] 'River Exploration in Labrador'. *Geographical Journal*. Vol. 75. No. 2. London.

of Labrador, in the opposite direction, to Nova Scotia. Bjarne's first land.

What is most interesting about this report, however, is the fact that it took Leiv two *doegr* to cover this distance. This is the same amount of time that we found Bjarne had taken earlier to cover the same distance from Nova Scotia to the southern coast of Labrador. Bjarne sailed from the south to the north with a southwesterly wind, and Leiv sailed from the north to the south with a northeasterly wind. The account of Leiv's voyage adduces strong evidence that this distance, with favorable winds, could be covered within two *doegr*, and lends strong support to the theory advanced above in respect of this stage of Bjarne's voyage. It is highly unlikely that Leiv made a stop at Newfoundland. If he had spent time ashore he would have taken more than two *doegr* for the passage. More important, if he had enough wind to sail from Labrador to Scatari in two *doegr*, which would require a strong wind, he certainly would not try to land on Newfoundland, since to carry him at that speed the wind would be in a northeasterly direction and the coast of Newfoundland would be a lee-shore. This would mean that the recent important discoveries of traces of Viking settlements in Newfoundland by Mr. and Mrs. Ingstad cannot be regarded as the remains of Leiv's *Budir*. These must be remains from other expeditions from Greenland, or from the time of Landa-Rolf, who colonized Newfoundland (1289-95) with the backing of the Norwegian king.

Having sailed down to Cape Race, and now entering on the second part of his two *doegr* voyage from Markland to Vineland, Leiv would alter course to the west, and remembering what he had heard of Bjarne's passage he would expect to see a coastline impeding his progress after about one *doegr*. We should remember that Leiv, unlike Bjarne, was exploring. Bjarne hastened eastward, keeping carefully away from the coast, searching for a clear passage to the north. Leiv, no doubt, sailed closer to the land, not only to observe its features, but because now it would be affording some protection from the northeast wind. Bearing in mind Bjarne's account he would set off over the stretch of water (Cabot Strait) that he knew lay between Bjarne's second and first lands. The alteration of course may have been decided after he had passed Miquelon Island, when there did not seem to be any more land to the north.

Thus he bore down on Nova Scotia, and came to an island which 'lay north of the mainland', where they went ashore. The only island that lies on this route and otherwise fits in with the description is Scatari. Bjarne and his crew had probably noted this island when they sailed away from their first land, and remembered it as the point from which, after allowing a respectful distance, they had made their first unsuccessful attempt to edge northward. But here it must be asked why Leiv did not go ashore on the Nova Scotian mainland. It would seem far more interesting to investigate the mainland itself than this insignificant little island off the coast. Here we must observe that Leiv had sailed for two *doegr* with a strong northeasterly wind. This wind had naturally caused rough seas on the ocean with high waves breaking on beaches exposed to the north and east, and it would have been impossible to approach this rocky coast. In order to get an impression of the land and the vegetation, they had to remain content with going ashore on this island and from it observing Nova Scotia, which was the northern part of the land they later named Vineland.

The northeasterly wind and high seas would not have prevented them from landing on Scatari, for on the south side of the island there is a large bay (Tin Cove) which would provide a very good harbor for a Viking ship under those weather conditions. The report of the journey indicates that the weather was good when they went ashore on the island. It would seem natural for Leiv to sail to the east of Scatari, since it would be obvious to him that there would be shallow waters and rocks between the island and the mainland. An experienced seaman would therefore most certainly sail to the east of the island. Soon after having

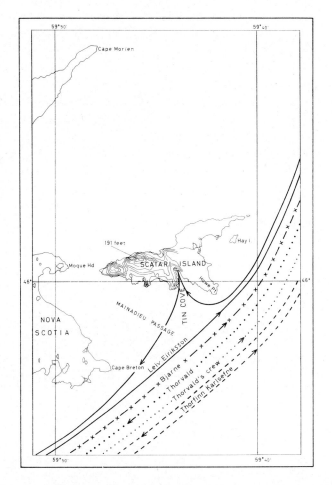

passed Scatari, he would see that, on the south side of the
island, there was a bay which could afford him a good place
for landing. With a northeast wind Leiv had only to make
his men trim the sail and he could then sail directly into
this harbor. It would thus be very simple to land on Scatari.

On this island, on which the highest point is about 200
feet, they had a good view over to the coast of Nova Scotia,
of the coast northwestward over toward the Gulf of
St. Lawrence, as well as along the east coast southward toward the present Halifax region. There on the island of

61

Scatari they had the opportunity to discuss which way to take from there — either westward along the north coast of Nova Scotia or toward the south along the east coast. With the northeasterly wind they had fair wind in both directions. However, in northern lands, the prospect of settling on a northern coast would not be so inviting when there was access to more southern regions. When standing on the peak of Scatari and weighing up the choice between the north coast of Nova Scotia and the more southern regions of America, the latter would surely be preferred. Leiv preferred the south. He sailed at once and continued until they reached a 'sound which lay between the island and the cape which ran north from the mainland'.

On the south side of the Gulf of St. Lawrence there are no geographical features that fit this description. The only area that can be identified with the account in the saga is Cape Cod, with the Barnestable Peninsula, Martha's Vineyard and Vineyard Sound. Let us take the saga as a guide and see what can be discovered.

As Bjarne had seen only the eastern end of Nova Scotia, Leiv and his men were the first Europeans to see the American coast from Halifax to Falmouth. We can imagine that they were eagerly watching the land, sailing as close as possible without risk for the expedition. They passed New Brunswick and Maine without going ashore, as Leiv always decided to keep on sailing further south, along the coast. At last they would run into Cape Cod Bay and Leiv would discover that he was in a broad cul-de-sac. He would have to sail north again, inside the bay, along the coast to Cape Cod. So he would discover that the *ness* (cape) pointed north from the mainland. On the east coast of Cape Cod there is no harbor. So he had to continue at least till he could find one.

The saga says: '*Stefnudu i vestrætt fyrir nesit'*. That means that they had come to the south point of Monomoy Island and laid their course west. '*Ok sigldu i sund þat, er lá milli eyjarinnar ok ness þess, er norðr er gekk af landinu.*' ('And sailed into the sound which lay between the island and that cape which ran north from the mainland.') With a course west from Monomoy Point they would sail right into Vineyard Sound (Falmouth). From East Falmouth the distance across this typical sound to Martha's Vineyard is so small that the houses that now stand on the island are easily visible. The 'lake' to which Leiv Eiriksson brought his ship and which they used as a harbor could very well be Waquoit Bay, a lagoon which is exactly like the one described in the saga. There is a short river flowing out of the lake. It resembles the *Hop* Lagoon which is described in Thorfinn Karlsefne's saga (see p. 88) and which he used as a harbor. In *Hop* the tide had to be quite high before the ship could float up into the lake. Likewise Leiv took his ship first into the river and later into the lake. In Falmouth there are several bays which could be used as harbors.

The shallow waters are a prominent feature of Vineyard Sound. What the saga says about ebb and flow indicates the shore in Waquoit Bay. A small river runs out of Waquoit Bay, which is a lake, just as described in the saga. Leiv took his ship first into the river and later into the lake. This suggests a shallow river, where they had to wait for the tide to rise, in order to bring the ship into the lake. Waquoit Bay has a depth of three to eight feet at low water, which would have been deep enough for Leiv's ship.

The information about the salmon is very interesting. Clearly the salmon could swim into the lake if the ship could float into it. The *Falmouth Fishing Guide,* with map, shows that salmon are still found in three small lakes, Peter's Pond, Mashpee Pond, and Ashume Pond, around Waquoit Bay. The saga is also accurate when it states that the salmon in Falmouth were bigger than the salmon they had seen earlier. In Greenland there is only *Salmo alpinus,* which seldom attains a weight of more than 10-12 pounds, while the salmon in the American rivers, *Salmo Salar,* may be 40-50 pounds.[21] Many scholars have claimed that the information about the salmon was a proof that the sagas

[21] Tornöe, op. cit., p. 82.

about the Vineland voyages were only fables. After investigating the Greenland salmon, we can rather take it as an indication that the sagas about Leiv Eiriksson are correct.

Finally, in conclusion to this account of the course taken by Leiv, and to give the student of Icelandic a sample of the source, here is part of the *Flateyarbok*'s original Icelandic text, recounting Leiv's voyage from Scatari to Falmouth:

... 'Siðan fóru þeir til skips sins, ok sigldu i sund þat, er lá milli eyjarinnar ok ness þess, er norðr gekk af landinu; stefndu i vestrætt fyrir nesit; þar var grunnsæfi mikit at fjöru sjófar, ok stóð þá uppi skip þeirra, ok var þá lángt til sjófar at sjá frá skipinu. En þeim var svá mikil forvitni á at fara til landsins, at þeir, nentu eigi þess at biða, at sjór fèlli undir skip þeirra, ok runnu til lands, þar er á ein fell or vatni einu; en þegar sjór fèll undir skip þeira, þá toku þeir bátinn, ok rèru til skipsins, ok fluttu þat upp i ána, siðan i vatnit, ok köstuðu þar akkerum, ok báru af skipi huðföt sin, ok gerðu þar búðir; toku þat rád siðan, at buast þar um þann vetr, ok gerðu þar hús mikil. Hvorki skorti þar lax i ánni nè i vatninu, ok stærra lax enn þeir hefði fyrr seð. þar var svá góðr landskostr, at þvi er þeim syndist, at þar mundi eingi fenaðr foðr þurfa á vetrum; þar kvomu eingi frost á vetrum, ok litt rènuðu þar grös. Meira var þar jafndægri enn á Grænlandi eðr Islandi; Sól hafði þar eyktarstað ok dagmálastað um skamdegi.' (See translation p. 50, above)

Leiv's sun observation in Falmouth

By considering the description of the place in the saga, we have now located Leiv's *Budir* in Falmouth, and yet we have not taken into account Leiv Eiriksson's sun observation, which offers the most important evidence of the location of Leiv's *Budir*. We will now see how Leiv's sun observation can fit into the latitude of Falmouth.

Leiv Eiriksson was the first astronomer in America. We will now try to find what kind of an astronomer he was. We know that he had no chronometer, no chart, and no compass. He knew that the Earth was a globe turning from west to east. The Norsemen had seen the Midnight Sun in Norway as well as in Greenland. The expedition of the priests to northern Greenland observed the height of the sun both at noon and at midnight on Jacobmes day, in order to find the latitude of the place.[22]

Leiv Eiriksson knew that if he observed the height of the sun at noon, or sunrise, or sunset on a certain day, he could approximately determine the latitude of the place. He could report his observations to King Olav Trygvason, his sponsor, so that the king and his men could compare Leiv's observations with similar observations from Norway, England, France, and Russia, where the king and his men had lived for some time. In that way they could try to assess the position of Vineland. For this reason the observation of the sun was very important, and we can imagine that it was one of the main observations Leiv made. Probably, he made these observations of the sun throughout the time he was in Falmouth. At least it is unlikely that Leiv observed the sun only on the shortest day of the year.

But perhaps he mentioned his finding on the shortest day because it is so easy to understand and so easy to remember. Leiv stated: *'Meira var þar jafndægri enn á Grænlandi eðr Islandi; Sól hafði þar eyktarstað ok dagmálastað um skamdegi'.* ('Day and night were more equally divided [more like equinox] there [at Leiv's *Budir*] than in Greenland and Iceland; the sun rose at breakfast time (*dagmálastað*) and set at supper time (*eyktarstað*), on the shortest day of the year.')

In the time of Leiv Eiriksson, everyone knew the mark on the horizon for the sun at breakfast time (*dagmálastað*) and supper time (*eyktarstað*). Further explanation was not necessary. But since the development of the chronometer, the meaning of *'Dagmálastað'* and *'Eyktarstað'* has been forgotten. Scholars have held very different opinions about the meaning of these two Norse words.

Arngrimur Jónsson (1568-1648) suggested that *eykt* was the same as noon (Latin, *nona hora*, the 9th hour of the day, or 3 p.m.) in the Icelandic Canon Law in Grágás. The

[22] Tornöe, op. cit., pp. 69, 89; also Almar Næss: *Hvor lå Vinland,* pp. 126-27, 232.

length of the shortest day at Leiv's *Budir* should, accordingly, be six hours, and the *budir* would be at 58° 20′ in Labrador. But this place is quite unlike the place described in the saga. Labrador has no grapes.

Thormod Torfæus (1636-1719) found another statement in the law in Grágás: '*þá er eykt er utsuðrs — ætt er deilld i þridiunga ok hefir solinn geingna tvo luti enn einn ogeingin.*' According to this, *eykt* should be about 4 p.m. and the shortest day at Leiv's *Budir* of about eight hours. He located Leiv's *Budir* at 49° in Newfoundland. Dr. Vigfusson and Dr. Finsen both held the same opinion, which they based on the so-called *Biskupaeykt*. But these laws were made for different purposes and they were made at least a hundred years after the time of Leiv Eiriksson, so he did not know anything about them and could not have used them. All locations of Leiv's *Budir* based on these rules are therefore incorrect.

On the other hand, Páll Vidalin and Finnur Jónsson found Snorre Sturlason's Calendar, which was used to determine the first day of winter by observing the sunset in *eyktarstað*, just as Leiv Eiriksson did at Leiv's *Budir*. G. M. Gathorne-Hardy[23] claims that 4.30 p.m. is found by observation to be the time for sunset at the same latitude as Snorre's farm in Iceland, Reykholt, on the first day of winter. Though it is not certain that Snorre's *eyktarstað* was equal to Leiv's *eyktarstað* it is of interest to observe the result of incorporating it in Leiv's observation in Falmouth. For the sake of brevity, we quote Snorre Sturlason's Calendar: 'Autumn lasts from the equinox (Sept. 21) till the sun sets in *eyktarstað* (Oct. 21). Winter till the equinox (March 21). Spring till the May moving day (May 21), Summer till the equinox (Sept. 21).'[24]

Eyktarstað is the point on the horizon where the sun set on the 21st of October as Snorre watched it from his farm

---

[23] *The Norse Discoverers of America,* p. 216.

[24] Quoted from Snorre's *Edda* in Almar Næss, op. cit., p. 50. See also op.cit., pp. 142-43 for an explanation of why Snorre's spring extends into May.

at Reykholt. If we measure the angle on the horizon from south to that point we find it is 67.5 degrees. When Leiv Eiriksson observed the sunset in Leiv's *Budir* (Falmouth), he found that the sun set in *eyktarstað* (67.5 degrees from south) not on the 21st of October as in Iceland, but on the 21st of December, the shortest day of the year. Just as Snorre determined the first day of winter, Leiv determined the winter solstice by observing the sunrise and the sunset. For such an exact observation one supposes that the sunset had to be over the ocean. The south shore of Barnestable Peninsula is the only area on the east coast that is possible. This is further evidence that Leiv's *Budir* was at Falmouth or Waquoit Bay. Here the sun rises and sets over the ocean. Here Leiv could find the meridian (N-S line) through his position by dividing the angle on the horizon from *dagmálastað* (sunrise) to *eyktarstað* (sunset). Or he could find *eyktarstað* by setting off an angle of 135 degrees on the horizon from sunrise. We should perhaps add that in making these calculations it is thought most likely that both Snorre and Leiv observed the upper edge of the sun rising above or disappearing below the horizon.

How Leiv contrived to observe the sun without instruments is not known, but he might have done it this way: he could make a center for his observations by driving a stick into the ground, e.g. at the east side of Waquoit Bay. Over this stick he could aim at the rising sun and at a proper distance drive down another stick in line from the center of the sun. The angles between the sticks he could divide with the help of a rope instead of a compass, and thus construct the meridian through the center, etc. This would be easier than observing the height of the sun at noon. He could then use other sticks to determine the difference between the points on the horizon for sunrise and sunset day by day, e.g. from the equinox to the winter solstice. After that day the sun would start to move back day by day as the length of the day increased, all the way to the summer solstice. Especially at midsummer it would be easy to notice that the day was much longer in Green-

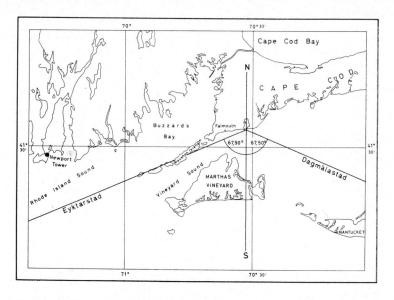

land and Iceland than at Leiv's *Budir* in Vineland. '*Meira var þar jafndægri enn à Grænlandi eðr Islandi.*' This indicates that Leiv's *Budir* was located much further south than the latitude of Labrador or Newfoundland.

It can be ascertained from modern maps that the latitude of Snorre's farm at Reykholt is 64° 40′, and that of Falmouth is 40° 33′.

Chronometers enable us to observe that the sun moves approximately 15 degrees on the horizon in one hour. *Eyktarstað* (67.5 degrees) means 4.5 hours or 4.30 p.m. in Iceland, at the latitude 64° 40′, on Oct. 21.

In Falmouth *Eyktarstað* (67.5 degrees) means 4.5 hours or 4.30 p.m. on the shortest day of the year (Dec. 21), according to Leiv Eiriksson's observations of the sun. Are his observations correct? Were they made at Falmouth?

According to the *Sandy Hook Pilot*'s tide table the time for sunset in Falmouth on Dec. 21, the shortest day of the year, is 4.31 p.m.

The difference in time is one clock minute, between the time reckoned according to Leiv's observation (4.30 p.m.) and the time given in the tide table (4.31 p.m.).

We know that the sun moves one degree on the horizon in 4 clock minutes. The deviation in Leiv Eiriksson's observation seems to be only ¼ of a degree on the horizon — a surprisingly accurate result.

It is unlikely that Leiv Eiriksson knew anything about refraction or any formula for reckoning the latitude. For that reason it would merely be confusing to refer to modern astronomy. But information may be found in Almar Næss's *Hvor lå Vinland*, especially pages 51-55.

An attempt to ascertain more precisely the point where Leiv made his observations at Falmouth reveals that there were only two favorable places. The first point is near the river flowing out of Waquoit Bay. Perhaps Leiv's houses were situated there. There he would get a free bearing to the sunrise, but the bearing to the sunset on the shortest day of the year might possibly be obstructed by Naushon Island. On the other hand, the distance to this low island is about 15 miles, so that it may well be below the horizon. However, observation of the summer sunset from this point might be hampered since the land to the west and north is 50-100 feet high.

The best location for observing the sun is Woods Hole. From this point there is an unobstructed view of the horizon, and the bearing to the sunset, on the shortest day of the year, passes just west of Block Island. Therefore it is most likely that Leiv made his sun observation at Woods Hole.

The wild grapes in Vineland

The most controversial issue in Leiv Eiriksson's report is the finding of the wild grapes. Nansen, perhaps inspired by Moltke Moe, used the narrative about the grapes to 'prove' that the whole saga is a fable.

Gustav Storm (*Studies on the Vineland Voyages,* 1887) attempted to show that Leiv Eiriksson or the saga writer did not know anything about grapes. Storm says that they claimed to have found the grapes in 'spring' and that they cut the vines for lumber to be used in Greenland. It was also suggested that the Turk got drunk by eating the grapes.

Gustav Storm assumed that Leiv Eiriksson came only to Newfoundland and Nova Scotia, where there are no grapes, thereby laying upon himself the onus of proving that the grapes in the saga were just a misunderstanding.

Other writers who contended that the Vineland expeditions went into the Gulf of St. Lawrence suggested that they perhaps found some kind of berries which were growing there and that they called them grapes. This idea appealed to many students.

Sven Söderberg (Vinland, in *Snællposten*, 1910) found in a dictionary that *vin* could mean 'meadow', or 'grassland', and need not necessarily refer to vines and grapes: the question of berries need not arise. Söderberg's theory was adopted by several of the writers who were endeavoring to locate Vineland in Hudson Bay, Labrador, or Newfoundland. Some of these make the point their key argument. Yet a glance at the Icelandic text makes it perfectly clear that *vinvið ok vinber* refers to vines and grapes and here has nothing to do with meadows or grassland.

The question whether Leiv Eiriksson did indeed find grapes in Vineland, or only berries or meadows, should be answered once for all.

I have made a special study of the wild grapes which still grow in many places in America. Wild grapes were growing among birch and peach trees at a place where I worked for two years. I have also seen great numbers of grapes growing wild in the American woods.

Wherever some of the old forests still stand, there are usually many wild grapes growing up along the trees, hanging under the branches, sometimes all the way to the top. These clusters growing on maple, birch, elm, or oak are clusters of grapes, not of berries. So it seems that Söderberg's theory can be discounted and the possibility of a confusion with berries dismissed.

We must remember that it was not one of the Greenlanders who found the grapes, but a Turk who had grown up in Turkey, where there was no lack of grapes. The first man to doubt that they really had found grapes was Leiv Eiriksson himself. He asked: 'Is that true?' 'Certainly it is true', the Turk replied.

There seems to be no reason to doubt that Leiv's expedition found grapes in Falmouth and on Martha's Vineyard. We know that when these areas were settled later, such an abundance of grapes was found there that the island was given the name Martha's Vineyard. Even today it is not difficult to find wild grapes in the American woods.

Leiv Eiriksson's crew found so many grapes, the story goes, that they filled their pinnace (afterboat) with the fruit. Most writers have ignored this important information in the saga because it does not fit in with their attempts to locate Leiv's *Budir* in Labrador, Newfoundland or Nova Scotia. Yet the events described are well within the bounds of possibility. Let us say that Leiv divided his crew so that eighteen men went to gather grapes and eighteen worked in the camp. Let us suppose that each man cut down 100 pounds of vines and grapes. They could leave the grapes on the vines and cut them or fold them to a length of a yard or a little more. These lengths they could put on a double rope to a load of about 100 pounds to carry on their backs, as they do in Iceland and Norway with grass and hay. From experience, I know that 100 pounds would not be too much for a man to carry to the boat. In that way they could have loaded 1,800 pounds into the boat and filled it with vines and grapes as stated in the saga.

The next day this half of the crew would work in the camp. Then they could separate the grapes from the vines and make wine of the grapes. The cargo of the ship could have been the wine which they were able to produce, complemented with as much timber as the ship could take. Eighteen men gathered grapes every day during the season and the afterboat was full of grapes. The afterboat was a big boat, which indicates that they had gathered so many grapes that they may well have produced enough wine to store it for future use.

71

This possibility is confirmed by the report of Thorvald's expedition. After Thorvald's death his crew went back to Leiv's *Budir* for the winter. '. . . *ok (þeir) bjuggu þar þann vetr, ok fengu sèr vinber ok vinvið til skipsins.*' (Translation p. 77) This means that they gathered vines and grapes, not only to make wine to drink, but for the cargo of the ship.

All the evidence here points to an abundance of grapes near Leiv's *Budir*, which therefore cannot have been located in Labrador, Newfoundland, or Nova Scotia. Falmouth, in the vicinity of Martha's Vineyard, is a far more likely locality.

Both Leiv's crew and Thorvald's crew cut vines for the cargo of their ships. The Greenlanders probably had a great demand for baskets of different kinds and the vines most likely were used in basketry.

Finally, to conclude and document this examination of the wild-grape question, here is the relevant part of the Icelandic text:

'. . .þá mælti Leifr til hans: "Hvi vartu svá seinn, fostri minn, ok fráskili föruneytinu?" Han talaði þá fyrst lengi á þýrsku, ok skaut marga vega augunum, ok gretti sik; en þeir skildu eigi, hvat er han sagði. Hann mælti þá á norrænu, en stund leið. "Ek var geinginn eigi miklu leingra, en þó kann ek nokkur nýnæmi at segja; ek fann vinvið ok vinber."

' "Mun þat satt, fostri minn?" kvað Leifr. "At visu er þat satt," kvað hann, "þviat ek var þar fæddr, er hvorki skorti vinvið né vinber."

'Nú svófu þeir af þá nótt; en um morguninn mælti Leifr við háseta sina: "Nú skal hafa tvennar syslur fram, ok skal sinn dag hvort, lesa vinber, eðr höggva vinvið ok fella mörkina, svá at þat verði farmr til skips mins;" ok þetta var ráðs tekit. Svá er sagt at eptirbátr þeirra var fylldr af vinberjum. Nú var högginn farmr á skipit; ok er vorar, þá bjuggust þeir, ok sigldu burt, ok gaf Leifr nafn landinu eptir landkostum, ok kallaði Vinland . . .' (See translation pp. 50-51, above).

Conclusions

I cannot agree with the opinion expressed by Pohl[25] and Holand[26] that Follins Pond was the lake into which Leiv Eiriksson took his ship and beside which he built his *budir*. Leiv could not see Follins Pond from the ocean; nor could it be Bass River, since there is no harbor, and therefore it would be quite difficult to land there in foggy weather or in stormy weather from the east, south, or southwest. Neither can it be said that Bass River runs into a typical sound, since Nantucket is so far out that it cannot be seen from the mainland, and it offers very little protection against the ocean at Bass River. Thus, it is very doubtful that Leiv Eiriksson would have called it a 'sound', and still more doubtful that he would have settled down there for a whole year.

Quite different is Falmouth, protected by Martha's Vineyard, where they could go ashore or out to sea in all kinds of weather, since in that locality there are many outlets, lagoons, and harbors of the kind they needed. Waquoit Bay is clean, and the river runs into a typical sound. If they had investigated the land as far west as Falmouth, they would scarcely have settled in the mud and dirt at Bass River. Holand and Pohl point out Bass River as the river where Leiv Eiriksson brought his ship because they consider the river a major waterway to a large inland lake. But this is a misunderstanding. The Norsemen did not seek a large inland lake, but a lagoon near the coast, where they could easily go out for the daily fishing. We must keep in mind that at that time they did not have salt as a preservative for fish. Thus they had to go to sea to fish almost daily. From Follins Pond out to sea would be too far for daily ventures.

When I was at Bass River in the summertime, there was not a single boat around, but in Waquoit Bay several sailboats were sailing in the lake, and outside the lake were many boats of different kinds. This seems to indicate that

25 Op. cit., p. 49.
26 Op. cit., p. 41.

Falmouth is a more suitable place for boats than Bass River.

We have another piece of evidence which locates Leiv's *Budir* south of Cape Cod, or in Falmouth. Leiv's brother, Thorvald, spent the winter in Leiv's *Budir*. He traveled east and north and was stranded at *Kjalarnes* (Cape Cod).

Leiv's *Budir,* moreover, must have been east of Rhode Island. Thorfinn Karlsefne stopped for a while at Leiv's *Budir.* When he left, he went into the fjord of Rhode Island on his way south past Block Island and into Long Island Sound to Manhattan (see pp. 99 ff).

The conjecture of Pohl and Holand that Leiv Eiriksson sailed from southern Nova Scotia straight to Cope Cod without seeing land cannot be correct. Leiv could not set course for a cape which he did not know. As we have seen, since Bjarne had not reached farther south than Nova Scotia, he would not have been able to inform about Cape Cod. But even if Leiv had learned anything about Cape Cod, we can be sure that he would sail along the coast in order not to get lost, since he had no compass.

That Pohl and Holand have difficulty in identifying the island 'north of the mainland' with Cape Cod, is because they both name Newfoundland 'Helluland' (Bjarne's third land and Leiv's first land). So they push Markland over onto Nova Scotia. According to the saga, Markland should be Bjarne's second land and Leiv's second land. Markland fits Newfoundland and Labrador in all connections, but not Nova Scotia. We know that Nova Scotia fits Bjarne's first land and Leiv's third land in all respects, and thus was part of Vineland, but not of Markland. Nova Scotia is not a separate land but only the northern part of Leiv's third land, the land that Leiv named Vineland. North of Nova Scotia is the island (Scatari) where Leiv landed when he came to his third land, Vineland. But according to Holand and Pohl Nova Scotia should be Leiv's second land. Then where is his third land (Vineland)? That should be Cape Cod according to several scholars who think that Vineland is only the area where Leiv built his houses, but in the saga the settlement is named Leiv's *Budir* in Vineland,

and Vineland's northern border is the Gulf of St. Lawrence, and there was once a belief that its southern limit 'almost reaches the African islands';[27] and north of Cape Cod there is no island such as the saga says they landed on and looked around.

[27]Tornöe, op. cit., p. 215.

Thorvald's Expedition

In the *Flateyarbok* we read:

'Now there was much discussion of Leiv's expedition to Vineland, and Thorvald, his brother, thought that the exploration of the country had been confined to too narrow an area. So Leiv said to Thorvald, "Now you, my brother, may,if you desire, make use of my ship for a trip to Vineland: but I wish the ship to go first for the wood which Thori had on the reef." And this was done. Thereupon Thorvald prepared for this expedition, taking thirty men on the advice of Leiv, his brother. Afterward they made their ship ready and held out to sea, and there is no report of their voyage before they came to Vineland to Leiv's camp. There they laid up their ship, and remained quiet that winter, catching fish for their food.

'In the spring Thorvald told them to make ready their ship, and ordered the ship's pinnace with some of the crew to go to the west of the country and explore there during the summer. It seemed to them a fine wooded country, the trees coming close down to the sea, and there were white sands. There were many islands, and many shoals. They found no traces of either men or beasts, except that on an island to the west they found a wooden barn. Finding no further human handiwork they returned, and came to Leiv's camp in the autumn.

'The next summer Thorvald sailed to the east with his trading ship, and along the more northerly part of the country: then a sharp storm arose off a cape, so that they ran ashore, breaking the keel under their ship; so they made a long stay there to repair their vessel. Then Thorvald said to his companions, "Now I wish that we should raise up the keel here on the cape, and call it *Kjalarnes*", and so they did.

Afterward they sailed away thence and eastward along the coast and into the nearest fjord mouths, and to a headland which ran out there: it was all covered with wood. Then they moored their ship, and put out the gangway to land, and there Thorvald went ashore with all of his crew. Then he remarked, "This is a beautiful spot, where I should like to make my home." After this they returned to the ship, and saw on the sands inside the headland three humps, and on approaching they saw three canoes of skin, with three men beneath each. Thereupon they divided their party, and laid hands on all of them, except one who escaped with his canoe. They killed the eight, and afterward went back to the headland, when they saw inside the fjord some mounds, which they took to be dwelling-places. After this there came over them so great a heaviness that they could not keep awake, and they all fell asleep. Then came a cry from above them, so that they all woke up, and the cry was, "Awake, Thorvald, and all your company, if you value your life: and return to your ship with all your men, and leave the land with all speed." At that there came from within the fjord countless skin canoes, which made toward them. So Thorvald said, "We must set the war-shields over the side, and defend ourselves as well as we can, while assuming the offensive but little." So they did, but the savages, after shooting at them for a while, afterward fled away, each as quickly as he could. Then Thorvald asked his men if they were wounded at all; they said there were no casualties.

' "I have got a wound under my arm", said he; "an arrow flew between the gunwale and the shield under my arm and here it is, and it will be my death. Now my advice is that you prepare to go away as quickly as possible, after carrying me to that headland which I thought the best place to dwell in: maybe it was the truth that came into my mouth that I should stay there awhile. Bury me there with a cross at my head and at my feet, and call it Crossness hereafter forever". Greenland was by then converted, though Eirik the Red died before conversion.

'Now Thorvald died, but they carried out all his instructions, after which they went and met their companions, and told each other such tidings as they knew, and they stayed there that winter, gathering grapes and vines for their ships. Then in the spring they prepared to go back to Greenland, and arrived with their ship in Eiriksfjord, with great news to tell Leiv.'

After Bjarne's and Leiv's travels, the subsequent expedition to Vineland was under the leadership of Thorvald, Leiv's brother. About Thorvald's trip the *Flateyarbok* says: 'there is no report of their voyage before they came to Vineland to Leiv's camp.' This sentence verifies what we have pointed out earlier, namely that Leiv's *Budir* was in Vineland. As mentioned earlier, Thorvald must have followed the same route as Bjarne and Leiv — east of Newfoundland. Thorvald had resolved to sail around Vineland and make a full survey of the location and size of the land. It was of importance to him to discover the most advantageous conditions and resources of the new land, and to choose the best possible place to settle with his numerous followers.

Even in the first winter after Leiv had returned from Vineland to Greenland Thorvald suggested that the land had not been investigated extensively enough. Then Leiv said to Thorvald: 'Now you, my brother, may if you desire, make use of my ship for a trip to Vineland', and during the summer Thorvald went to Vineland with a crew of 30 men, as his brother had advised.

The saga does not mention anything more about this expedition until they reached Leiv's *Budir* (Falmouth) in Vineland. They remained there quietly during that winter and obtained their sustenance by means of fishing. But with the advent of spring, Thorvald ordered his crew to make their ship ready for a voyage; some of his men would sail in the larger of the ship's boats westward around the land during the summer to investigate it more extensively. '*Fara fyrir vestan landit*' means to travel westward around the land. This expression indicates that Thorvald had in mind that they would not have to sail so far before reaching the southern point of Vineland, whence they would be able, perhaps, to move up along the west coast of the land. With their meager knowledge of the actual situation, they had no reason for believing that Vineland was so very extensive. They were well informed about England, Ireland, and Iceland; and they knew that it was not so difficult with a large boat to sail around those lands during the summer. With this in mind, Thorvald gave the order to his men that they should sail westward around Vineland for the purpose of exploration.

During his summer in Vineland, Thorvald sailed in his merchant ship (the large ship) eastward and north around the land. Thorvald's intention may have been to sail the large ship toward the north (north around Nova Scotia) and then west around the land, while some of his men in the ship's large boat sailed around the land in the opposite direction. Eventually they were to meet each other at some point on the west coast of the island which they believed Vineland to be. If they did not meet as planned, they were to return to Leiv's *Budir* before the return of stormier weather with the fall. The expression, '*En at sumri odru*', must mean the summer after they arrived from Greenland, as Thorvald made the ship ready in the spring. I understand the saga to mean that both parties should explore the land simultaneously and in opposite directions. After Thorvald's death, his crew went back to Leiv's *Budir* and met their 'companions'. It is reasonable to assume that the companions were the boat crew coming back in the fall.

About those who went in the ship's larger boat westward around Vineland, the saga has a report. This report is the only written record that has come down to us about that long and remarkable journey. We must assume that they prepared for the trip in the winter and that they were on the move during spring, summer, and fall. At least Thorvald had his ship ready in the spring. As they prepared for the journey in the winter, we must suppose that they started as early in the spring as the weather permitted. The merchant ships from Norway to England used to start late in April. But this was a journey along the American coast. It is not unlikely that the preparations for the voyage were based on a period of about five months, from May to October.

We may take it for granted that they were on the move

only during the daylight hours, since they would sail along the coast in order to get a fair view of the land, but they did not go inland for exploratory purposes. The latter statement is supported by the fact that they did not see any traces of human beings or animals. Their task was to try to sail around Vineland.

How far could they sail and row on a round trip of five months in the summer. To Florida? To Texas? To Mexico? We recall that Bjarne sailed from Nova Scotia to Baffin Land and Greenland in nine days. In 1896 Harbo and Lund *rowed* (they had no sail) from New York to Le Havre, France, in a boat 18 feet long, in 56 days. At least the Norsemen learned that Vineland was an immense land.

We will now try to trace Thorvald's voyage from Leiv's *Budir* to Crossness, where he was killed by the Indians and buried.

Thorvald had spent the winter in Leiv's *Budir* (Falmouth). From there he started on this journey and sailed to *Kjalarnes,* where he ran aground. Repairs took a long time, we are told; when they were completed they sailed away over to the coast of Massachusetts and into the nearest fjord mouth.

Later, both Thorhall and Karlsefne were to sail over the same course. Coming from the south, Thorhall sailed 'north past... *Kjalarnes* and tried to beat westward...' Karlsefne later sailed 'with one ship to search for Thorhall Veidiman ... north past *Kjalarnes* and steered then westward on...'

Thorvald sailed east and north of the land. This can refer to his planned voyage north of Nova Scotia and as far west as he could penetrate. But it can also indicate his course from Leiv's *Budir* (Falmouth) to *Kjalarnes* (Cape Cod). In this case it will be seen that the direction mentioned in the saga is correct. From Falmouth to Monomoy Point is east, and from there to Cape Cod is due north. After having raised the broken keel of their ship on the Cape as a sailing mark, they sailed 'from there [Cape Cod] into the nearest fjord mouth'.

The nearest 'fjord mouth' to Cape Cod is the entrance

to Plymouth Harbor. The saga does not say a fjord — but a 'fjord mouth'. This is a vivid description. From the map (p. 83) it may be seen that the area looks like the mouth of a troll or of a giant. In Norway they still name such a bay 'a fjord mouth' or a fjord *gap*. Plymouth Harbor is not a regular fjord, and would be called a 'fjord mouth' by the Norse. 'They continued to a headland [*höfda*] which ran out there; it was all covered with wood.'

When sailing into this fjord mouth one can see Captain's Hill straight ahead. This headland is exactly what was called in old Norse *höfda*; the word is still common in Iceland and Norway today. The *höfda* was covered with wood, and so is Captain's Hill today. It is the only place where they could expect water deep enough to float their ship right up to shore so that they could put out a gangway. That is just what the saga says they did.

'Then they moored their ship, and put the gangway to land, and there Thorvald went ashore with all of his crew. Then he remarked. "This is a beautiful spot where I should like to make my home."'

The place fits exactly with the saga's description. Captain's Hill, where they landed, is 200 feet high. From there they could see the beautiful areas around Plymouth, where there would be plenty of land for homesteads for Thorvald and his crew. There is an excellent harbor, and Plymouth is not too far from Falmouth, where Leiv Eiriksson, Thorvald's brother, had made a homestead for himself and his crew. In a few years, Thorvald could expect to have Norse farms all the way from Plymouth to Falmouth. But then there was a dramatic development.

'After this they returned to the ship, and saw on the sands inside the headland three humps, and on approaching they saw three canoes of skin, with three men beneath each.'

This is the first time that white men met with Indians. Up to that day the Norsemen believed there were no people in America.

There are sands inside the headland of Captain's Hill.

The description of the place fits in all details. From Captain's Hill it is easy to see over to Plymouth and Plymouth Harbor and it would not be too far away to see the Indian huts which the party described as mounds.

After this comes the piece of supernatural fiction with the sleepiness and the cry, 'Awake Thorvald!' But except for this little story there is no fiction in this narrative. The cry could in any case have come from a sentinel. The whole story registers so precisely with the fjord mouth, Plymouth Harbor and Cape Cod, that no man who had not taken part in the events could have described the setting of this story.

Some people have found further evidence for the fictitiousness of the saga's account of Thorvald's voyage in the mention of a Thorvald in the later expedition of Karlsefne recounted in the *Hauksbok,* but the Thorvald referred to in the *Hauksbok* account (p. 85) was probably Thorvard, who was connected by marriage with Eirik the Red. The narrative in the *Flateyarbok* will have to be regarded as the definitive record of Thorvald's expedition to Vineland. There can be very little doubt that Thorvald was buried on Captain's Hill, and that this little headland is *Krossanes.* [28]

[28] It is possible that we still possess the arrow which killed Thorvald Eiriksson. The Danish archeologist Aage Roussell has excavated the farm of Sandnes in Greenland. This farm belonged to Thorstein, the brother of Thorvald. In the graveyard on the farm, Aage Roussell found an arrowhead of Indian origin, now in the collection of the Copenhagen Museum. See *Medd. om Grönland* 88, II, pp. 106-07. In my opinion this arrow (see Pl. III, p. 48) could be the one which killed Thorvald Eiriksson.

Thorvald pulled out the arrow from under his arm and said: '...here it is, and it will be my death.' (See p. 77 above) The crew probably brought this Indian arrow to Thorstein in Sandnes as a proof that it was the Indians who killed Thorvald, and the arrow would also be a last souvenir of Thorvald in Greenland. The Greenlanders at times buried symbols for people who disappeared on voyages, e.g. a stick with the name of the person and where he or she died. The Indian arrow could very well have served as the symbol of Thorvald. His brother Thorstein fitted out an expedition in order

(cont. p. 84)

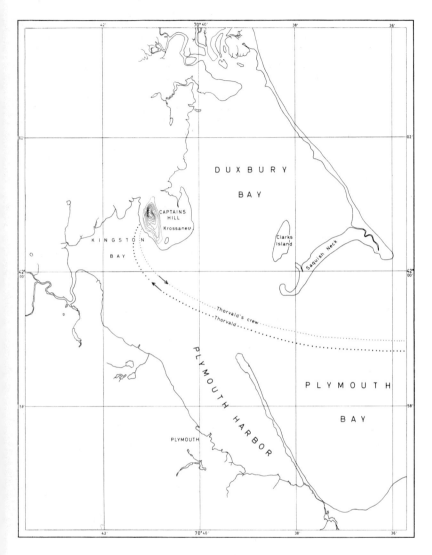

To sum up, Thorvald was an ambitious explorer. With the intention of circumnavigating Vineland, he dispatched the big boat with a part of his crew on a survey of the east coast of America on a round trip of at least five months, since they started in the spring and returned in the fall.

Thorvald gave the names *Kjalarnes* (Keelness) to Cape Cod, and *Krossanes* (Crossness) to Captain's Hill. Thorvald also erected the first sailing mark on the American coast by raising the keel of his ship on Cape Cod. He was the first white man to see the Indians in America, and also the first white man to give his life in America.

Confirmation of the saga about Thorvald is to be found in the report of Thorfinn Karlsefne's voyage.

'. . . peir réru til lands, ok fundu par á nesinu kjöl af skipi, ok kölludu par Kjalarnes; eir kölludu ok strandirnar Furdustrandir, pviat lángt var med at sigla.' (See translation, p. 86, below)

Karlsefne found the keel which Thorvald had left on *Kjalarnes*. They also used the name *Kjalarnes* which Thorvald had given to Cape Cod. There can be little doubt that the saga about Thorvald's voyage is a correct account.

(footnote 28 cont.)

to bring home the body of Thorvald, but did not succeed in finding Vineland, as mentioned in the *Flateyarbok*.

It is not unlikely that this Indian arrow is the one which killed Thorvald; but we cannot be sure. Thorstein Eiriksson was married to Gudrid the Fair and when he died, Gudrid married Thorfinn Karlsefne, and went with him to Vineland. When they returned from Vineland, most likely Thorfinn, Gudrid and their son Snorre went to her farm, Sandnes. Thorfinn had several battles with the Indians, so possibly Thorfinn brought the Indian arrow to Sandnes. But we have never heard that Thorfinn had such an arrow. Thorvald, however, and his crew had the Indian arrow, so most likely we have the arrow which killed Thorvald.

Thorfinn Karlsefne's Exploration
of America

From the *Hauksbok* we read:

'At this time there was much discussion at Brattahlid during the winter about a search for Vineland the Good, and it was said that it would be a profitable country to visit; Karlsefni and Snori resolved to search for Vineland, and so the project was much talked about; so it came that Karlsefni and Snori made ready their ship to go and look for the country in the summer. The man named Bjarni, and Thorhall, who have already been mentioned, joined the expedition with their ship, and the crew which had accompanied them. There was a man named Thorvald [evidently Thorvard] who was connected by marriage with Eirik the Red. He also went with them, and Thorhall who was called the Hunter; he had been long engaged with Eirik as hunter in the summer, and had many things in his charge. Thorhall was big and strong and dark, and like a giant: he was rather old, of a temper hard to manage, taciturn and of few words as a rule, cunning but abusive, and he was always urging Eirik to the worse course. He had had little dealings with the faith since it came to Greenland. Thorhall was rather unpopular, yet for a long time Eirik had been in the habit of consulting him. He was on the ship with Thorvald's men, for he had a wide experience of wild countries. They had the ship which Thorbjorn had brought out there, and they joined themselves to Karlsefni's party for the expedition, and the majority of the men were Greenlanders. The total force on board their ships was 160 men. .. [After this] they sailed away to the Western Settlement and the Bear Isles. They sailed away from the Bear Isles with a northerly wind. They were at sea two *doegr*. Then they found land, and rowing ashore in boats they examined the country, and found there a quantity of flat stones, which were so large that two men could easily have lain sole to sole on them: there were many arctic foxes there. They gave the place a name, calling it Helluland. Then they sailed for two *doegr* with a north wind, and changed their course from south to southeast, and then there was a land before them on which was much wood and many beasts. An island lay there off-shore to the southeast, on which they found a bear, and they called it Bjarney [Bear Island], but the land where the wood was they called Markland [woodland].

'Then when two *doegr* were passed they sighted land, up to which they sailed. There was a cape where they arrived. They beat along the coast and left the land to starboard. It was a desolate place, and there were long beaches and sands there. They rowed ashore, and found there on the cape the keel of a ship, so they called the place *Kjalarnes:* they gave the beaches also a name, calling them *Furdu-strandir* [the Wonder Beaches] because the sail past them was long. Next the country became indented with bays, into one of which they steered the ships.

'Now when Leiv was with King Olav Trygvason and he commissioned him to preach Christianity in Greenland, the king gave him two Scots, a man called Hake and a woman Hekja. The king told Leiv to make use of these people if he had need of speed, for they were swifter than deer: these people Leiv and Eirik provided to accompany Karl-sefni. Now when they had coasted past *Furdustrandir* they set the Scots ashore, telling them to run southward along the land to explore the resources of the country and come back before three days were past... They cast anchor and lay there in the meantime. And when three days were past they came running down from the land, and one of them had in his hand a grape cluster while the other had a wild [lit: self-sown] ear of wheat. They told Karlsefni that they thought they had found that the resources of the country were good. They received them into their ships, and went their way, till the country was indented by a fjord. There was an island outside the fjord. They took the ships into the fjord. There was an island, and about it there were long sounds [*Straumar miklir*], so they called it *Straumsey*. There were so many birds on the island that a man's feet could hardly come down between the eggs. They held along the fjord, and called the place *Straumsfjord*, and there they carried up their goods from the ships and prepared to stay. They had with them all sorts of cattle; and they explored the resources of the country. There were mountains there, and the view was beautiful. They did nothing but explore the country. There was plenty of grass there. They remained there for the winter, and the winter was severe, but they had done nothing to provide for it, and victuals grew scarce, and hunting and fishing deteriorated. They went out to the island, in the hope that this place might yield something in the way of fishing or jetsam. But there was little food to be obtained on it, though their cattle throve there well. After this they cried to God to send them something to eat, and their prayers were not answered as soon as they desired. . .

'Now they consulted about their expedition, and were divided. Thorhall the Hunter wished to go north by *Furdustrandir* and past *Kjalarnes,* and so look for Vineland, but Karlsefni wished to sail south (and off the east coast, considering that the region which lay more to the south was the larger), and it seemed to him the best plan to explore both ways. So then Thorhall made ready out by the island, and there were no more than nine men for his venture, the rest of the party going with Karlsefni. And one day as Thorhall was carrying water to his ship he drank it, and recited this verse:

> They flattered my confiding ear
> With tales of drink abounding here:
> My curse upon the thirsty land!
> A warrior, trained to bear a brand,
> A pail instead I have to bring,
> And bow my back beside the spring:
> For ne'er a single draught of wine
> Has passed these parching lips of mine.

'After this they set out and Karlsefni accompanied them by the islands. Before they hoisted their sail Thorhall recited another verse:

> Now let the vessel plough the main
> To Greenland and our friends again:
> Away, and leave the strenuous host
> Who praise this God-forsaken coast
> To linger in a desert land,
> And boil their whales in Furdustrand.

'Afterward they parted, and they sailed north past *Furdustrandir* and *Kjalarnes,* and tried to beat westward, but they were met by a storm and cast anchor ashore in Ireland, where they were much ill-treated and enslaved. There Thorhall died, according to the records of traders.

'Karlsefni coasted south with Snori and Bjarni and the rest of their party. They sailed a long time, till they came to a river which flowed down the land and through a lake into the sea. There were great shoals of gravel there in front of the estuary and they could not enter the river except at high tide. Karlsefni and his party sailed into the estuary, and called it *Hop*.

'They found there wild [lit: self-sown] fields of wheat wherever the ground was low, but vines wherever they explored the hills. Every brook was full of fish. They made pits where the land met high-water mark, and then when the tide ebbed there were fish [flounder] in the pits. There was a great quantity of animals of all sorts in the wood. They were there a fortnight, enjoying themselves, without noticing anything further: they had their cattle with them.

'And one morning early, as they looked about them, they saw nine skin canoes, on which staves were waved with a noise just like threshing, and they were waved with the sun. Then Karlsefni said, "What is the meaning of this?" Snori answered him, "Perhaps this is a sign of peace, so let us take a white shield and lift it in answer." And they did so. Then these men rowed to meet them, and, astonished at what they saw, they landed. They were swarthy men and ugly, with unkempt hair on their heads. They had large eyes and broad cheeks. They stayed there some time, showing surprise. Then they rowed away south past the cape.

'Karlsefni and his men had made their camp above the lake, and some of the huts were further inland while others were near the lake. So they remained there that winter. No snow fell, and their cattle remained in the open, finding their own pasture. But at the beginning of spring they saw early one morning a fleet of skin canoes rowing from the south past the cape, so many that the sea was black with them, and on each boat there were staves tied. Karlsefni and his men raised their shields, and they began to trade: the strange people wanted particularly to buy red cloth, in exchange for which they offered skins and grey furs. They wished also to buy swords and spears, but Karlsefni and Snori forbade this. The savages got for a dark skin a span's length of red cloth, which they bound round their heads. Thus things continued for a while, but when the cloth began to give out they cut it into pieces so small that they were not more than a finger's breadth. The savages gave as much for it as before, or more.

'It happened that a bull belonging to Karlsefni's party ran out of the woods, and bellowed loudly. This terrified the savages, and they ran out to their canoes, and rowed south along the coast, and there was nothing more seen of them for three consecutive weeks. But when that time had elapsed they saw a great number of the boats of the savages coming from the south like a rushing torrent, and this time all the staves were waved withershins, and all the savages yelled loudly. Upon this Karlsefni's men took a red shield and raised it in answer. The savages ran from their boats and thereupon they met and fought. There was a heavy rain of missiles; the savages had war-slings too. Karlsefni and Snori observed that the savages raised upon a pole a very large globe, closely resembling a sheep's paunch and dark in color, and it flew from the pole up on land over the party, and made a terrible noise where it came from. Upon this a great fear came on Karlsefni and his party, so they wished for nothing but to get away up-stream, for they thought that the savages were setting upon them from all sides; nor did they halt till they came to some rocks where they made a determined resistance. . .

'It now appeared to Karlsefni's party that though this country had good resources yet they would live in perpetual state of warfare and alarm on account of the aborigines. So they prepared to depart, intending to return to their own country. They coasted northward, and found five savages in skins sleeping by the sea; these had with them receptacles in which was beast's marrow mixed with blood. They concluded that these men must have been sent out from the country [outlawed], and they killed them. Later on they discovered a promontory and a quantity of beasts; the promontory had the appearance of a cake of dung, because the beasts lay there in the winter. Now they came to Straumsfjord, where there was plenty of everything.

'Some men say that Bjarni and Gudrid stayed there with a hundred men and went no further, while Karlsefni and Snori went south with forty men, staying no longer at *Hop* than a scant two months, and returning the same summer.

'They considered that those mountains which were at *Hop* and those which they now found were all one, and were therefore close opposite one another, and that the distance from *Straumsfjord* was the same in both directions. They were at *Straumsfjord* the third winter.

'At this time the men were much divided into parties, which happened because of the women, the unmarried men claiming the wives of those who were married, which gave rise to the greatest disorder. There Karlsefni's son Snori was born the first autumn, and he was there three winters when they left.

'On sailing from Vineland they got a south wind, and came to Markland. . .'

Comment on Karlsefne's exploration

With the purpose of making a closer examination of the remarkable expedition of Karlsefne, I have searched through the great historical records in *Grönlands Historiske Mindæsmerker*, as well as several variants of handwritten records, thus supplementing the main work with some additional and most important information.

We are told that 160 men accompanied Karlsefne when he sailed from the Eastern to the Western settlement and from there to *Bjarnöy* (or Disco Island).[29] They also took with them all kinds of domestic animals.

In accordance with the statements in two variant records, the expedition sailed from the north coast of Disco Island in a southerly direction for two *doegr* with a following wind from the north. Then they sighted land.

From the above it is easy to deduce that they sailed up along the west coast of Greenland, clear to the east- and north coast of Disco. All along that route they could find good harbors, where they could seek shelter in case of bad weather. From northern *Stromfjord* the expedition could sail most of the way along the leads inside the protective islands till they reached Disco Bay, where, too, they would be protected from all storms except those from the west. A well-protected waterway is found along the eastern and northern shores of Disco. Along this protected lead the expedition could find its way to the northwestern coast of that island. There they could stay until they got wind from the north. From there, with a favorable wind, they could

---

[29] Swanton (op. cit., p. 20) observes that Bjarnöy was a name often given to islands, and recalls that the Danish explorer Knut Graa established the fact that Disco was known as Bjarnöy.

90

reach westward to the edge of the pack-ice, along which they could sail southward to Cape Dyer in Baffin Land, in two *doegr*, at a speed of seven knots. At that point there is a mountain towering up to 7,000 feet. This peak would obviously have been an excellent marker for navigational direction in those waters, visible at 100 miles.

We can take it for granted that Thorhall Veidemann ('huntingman') and other sealers and fishermen were well acquainted with the coast of Greenland northward of Disco, and it was they who served as Karlsefne's pilots. Thorhall Veidemann had lived with Eirik the Red in Greenland for a long time. He was the manager of Eirik's farm during the winters and the leader of his hunting expeditions during the summers. That is, he was probably the captain of Eirik's ship when they were out hunting walrus, whales, seals and also polar bears in the summer. As a result of activities of this kind, he became well acquainted with the unsettled and desolate districts farther north in Greenland (and maybe Baffin Land).

He went along on the Vineland expeditions because he was so well acquainted with the coastal waters of Greenland; and this would be of immense importance if they headed north to Disco Island, and from there to Baffin Land, as suggested earlier. It seems quite clear that such a large waterborne expedition would not set out on such a risky and intricate voyage unless directed and guided by the best pilots available at the time. Very possibly Karlsefne had long with him men who had been with Bjarne Herjulfsson, Leiv Eiriksson and Thorvald Eiriksson, who were thus fairly well acquainted with the territories and ocean conditions clear west to Vineland.

The saga says that they reached the land (Baffin Land) and found many white foxes there. But the land was like a large flat stone. Therefore they called it Helluland (flatstone land) exactly as Leiv Eiriksson had done already. They were familiar with such terrain, which is found, for example, on the east coast of Greenland, where rain, ice, and storms have removed all gravel and soil that otherwise would have covered what is now only bare ground. It was this kind of bleak foothill, scoured bare by the ice, which was to Leiv Eiriksson the most prominent characteristic of the region, and earned for it the name of Helluland.

After a short inspection of the land, Karlsefne sailed for two *doegr* before a following wind from the north. Then the expedition changed course from south to southeast. Because of this navigational change, we can deduce that they were already across Hudson Strait and were at the northern point of Labrador (Markland). They would not have changed their course unless they were forced to do so because of the southeasterly direction of the coast of Labrador.

From Cape Dyer to Labrador the distance is about 360 miles. If we divide that by two *doegr,* of 48 hours, we find their average speed to have been 7.5 knots. This corresponds well with the fact that they reached Labrador in two *doegr* and thus had to change their direction. Their former course is stated to have been southward. Thus the account fits well. From Cape Dyer to the southern end of Cumberland Sound the coast leads to some extent in a southwesterly direction; but from that point to Labrador the course had to be southerly, as indicated in the saga. This account shows also that Karlsefne had been able to get correct observations from the sun both before and after he changed his course. Both courses correspond with the directions of the coasts north and south of Hudson Strait. This, therefore, is strong evidence in favor of the correctness and reliability of the saga account.[30]

Following the change of their course they found a forest-covered land with many wild animals. Thus they came to a new country — Labrador, or Markland. In one of the hand-

[30] G. Holand: op. cit., pp. 65-66. - 'But while a southeastern course might bring them to Africa, it would never bring them to Markland.'
Holand gets into these difficulties because his courses and sailing directions are entirely wrong. He puts Helluland on Newfoundland instead of Baffin Land, and so he pushes Markland over on to Nova Scotia.

written variants it is stated that they found a land covered with large trees. That would indicate that they had arrived in southern Labrador, where forests of large trees are found. There they found an island located in a southeasterly direction off the coast. On that island they killed a bear and called the place Bear Island (*Bjarney*); but the mainland they called Markland. Another variant adds: 'there, where the forest was.'

This corresponds very well with the southern coast of Labrador where the land is densely wooded; and Belle Isle is located off the coast in a southeasterly direction. As the direction of the coastline is the base for the direction to the island it is obvious that the coastline of the mainland had to be northeast to southwest, when the direction to the island was southeast. A glance at the map (p. 39) will reveal how perfectly it fits; and there is no other coastline with an island off it on the whole Labrador coast that fits this description.

This is the same coast where Leiv Eiriksson went ashore and which he named Markland, and it is the same coast that Bjarne sailed up to but where he did not make a landing. It is very likely that they killed a bear on Belle Isle, as the polar bears arrive there with the field-ice, and that they named the island accordingly.

We have now traced Karlsefne's route from Disco to Belle Isle. But now we must consider the question of their course after leaving Belle Isle. Did they sail through the Strait of Belle Isle into the St. Lawrence River, or along the east coast of Newfoundland? If they went through the Strait of Belle Isle they would certainly discover that Newfoundland was a separate land not connected with Labrador. Then they would have to add another land to Helluland, Markland, and Vineland in the west. But the saga mentions nothing like this. If they went into the St. Lawrence River they would also discover that Markland and Vineland were connected, and that they were not two separate lands, but one. However, the saga makes no reference to this fact, so it must be assumed that Karlsefne sailed east of Newfoundland, as did Bjarne and Leiv before him. 'From there [Belle Isle] they sailed southward along the coast for a long time until they came to a promontory [Cape Race on Newfoundland].' The land lay to the starboard. This indicates that they thought of a continuous coast for Labrador and Newfoundland and that they sailed toward the south along the east coast of Newfoundland. They could not have been sailing on the west side of Newfoundland, since, in sailing south, they had the land on the starboard side. 'Sailing for a long time' could mean from Belle Isle to Cape Race. Following the remarks about the land on the starboard side, the saga variants B and M state the following: 'Then when two *doegr* were passed, they sighted land, up to which they sailed. There was a cape where they arrived. ... It was a desolate place.' Also there were long shores and sand beaches.

This insertion above from the variants B and M indicates most definitely that they had sailed across from Cape Race, Newfoundland, to the coast of Nova Scotia. Then they tacked along the coast (*'Their beittu med landinu'*). This means they had a headwind and had to beat or tack. Two *doegr* from Cape Race to Nova Scotia with a headwind seems plausible enough for this span of water. When they had sailed down the entire length of the east coast of Newfoundland, their wisest and most natural course was westward from Cape Race along the south coast of Newfoundland and then over to Nova Scotia, crossing at the point where the distance is shortest.

One may conclude for certain that they would not have left the coast for as much as two *doegr* sailing without a compass, unless they had to sail across the outer part of the Gulf of St. Lawrence.

They continued to have the land on the starboard side. From this we may deduce that they had not sailed up into the Gulf of St. Lawrence, for then they would have had the land on the port side. Therefore, they had continued toward the south along the coast of Nova Scotia and then farther south. That they left there with the land on the starboard side could mean that they left Nova Scotia to sail across the Bay of Fundy and onward south along the coast, as had Leiv and Thorvald before them, until they came to a promontory. They halted, lowered a small boat, and landed on the promontory, where they found the keel of a ship. They accordingly named the place *Kjalarnes.*

The saga writer informs us that Karlsefne adopted the same name as that given to the ness by Thorvald. It was at *Kjalarnes,* as has been related above, that Thorvald had run aground and broken the keel of his ship. He then erected the first sailing mark in America by raising the broken keel on the point. Karlsefne's use of the name must mean that his expedition visited the same place, and there is a strong suggestion that he had with him some old members of Thorvald's crew who were familiar with earlier events.

They called the shorelines *Furdustrandir* (the long strands, or wonder strands) because it took so much time to sail along them. Now a strand, for our purposes, is a stretch of coastline uninterrupted by fjords, creeks, or inlets. A strand may have curved indentations, bays, but its length is judged by the distance between inlets. *Furdustrandir* describes long strands, bounded by inlets lying far from each other. *Furdustrandir* is plural, so there must have been at least two such long stretches. In my opinion the first 'strand' starts from the north point of Cape Cod and ends at Monomoy Point. This is a distance of about 37 miles of shoreline which looked unbroken when they saw it from the ocean. This is a very long strand. In Greenland they had nothing like *Furdustrandir.* In Norway there is only Jadarn which can be compared with the east side of Cape Cod.

From Monomoy starts another strand, which, seen from the ocean, seems unbroken all the way to Falmouth where the inlets bring it to an end. The length of this strand is about 30 miles, so it is no wonder that Karlsefne gave them the name *Furdustrandir* when he had to sail past them. '*peir kölludu ok strandirnar Furdustrandir pviat lángt var*

95

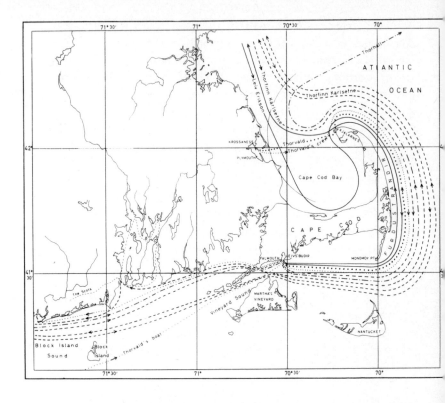

með at sigla. þá gerðist landit vákskorið . . .' The last sentence means that after *Furdustrandir* the land was indented with *vágar* — narrow bays or small harbors. This indicates Falmouth with its inlets (see the map).

Thorfinn Karlsefne, sailing south, mentioned *Furdustrandir* immediately after *Kjalarnes,* which places *Furdustrandir* south of Cape Cod. When Thorhall had left Manhattan for Greenland the saga states: 'Afterward they parted, and they sailed north past *Furdustrandir* and *Kjalarnes,* and tried to beat [*beita*] westward [*vestr fyri*] . . .' Which confirms that *Furdustrandir* were located south of Cape Cod. And Thorvald, sailing north, first passed *Furdustrandir* and afterward passed *Kjalarnes* (Cape Cod). This confirms also that *Kjalarnes* was Cape Cod, the only place where they could alter course from north to west.

By means of Thorfinn Karlsefne's saga we have been able to trace the route of the expedition from when they left the eastern settlement in Greenland until they landed at *Kjalarnes* in America. The next point where the expedition put in was at Leiv's *Budir* at East Falmouth on the south shore of Cape Cod.

We translate from the *Flateyarbok,* 'Eirik den Rödes saga', *Grönlands Historiske Mindesmærker* I', pp. 238-40:

'Karlsefne asked Leiv for his house in Vineland, but Leiv declared that he would lend his houses but not give them. Afterward they put out to sea with their ships, and arriving at Leiv's *Budir* safe and sound they carried up their baggage. They soon made a great and good catch, for a whale both large and good was stranded there, upon which they went to the whale and cut it up; they were then in no want of food.'

From this there can be no doubt that Karlsefne's expedition arrived at Leiv's *Budir,* though it is not related in the *Hauksbok.* As will be seen, the *Flateyarbok* leaves out all that the *Hauksbok* tells about the voyage from Greenland to *Kjalarnes,* and all that it tells till they had settled down in *Hop,* and started to fight with the Indians. Many scholars are of the opinion that there was a large 'Eirik Raude's Saga' and that both the *Flateyarbok* and the *Hauksbok* are only fragments preserved from the larger work.

We see that Karlsefne had received Leiv's consent to make use of his houses at Leiv's *Budir.* We must understand that both the people and the animals needed rest and plenty of food after the long voyage from Greenland to Leiv's *Budir.* Whalemeat is excellent food, and there was no want of fish.

There is no mention of Indians at Leiv's *Budir,* or at *Straumsey,* so it is easy to understand that the story about the bull and the Indians is associated with *Hop* in both books.

The reason why Leiv Eiriksson declined to give his houses at Leiv's *Budir* to Karlsefne may not be far to seek. It is probable that Leiv Eiriksson and his crew (35 men) had not only built the houses at Leiv's *Budir,* but had also occupied the land there themselves, and had lived on the farmland and woods around Falmouth. If they had not occupied the land there themselves, another man could come and occupy it and he could force Leiv Eiriksson to move his houses. We may assume that Leiv and his crew would not take that risk when they could acquire the whole area legally merely by announcing it as their property at the *Thing* (Parliament) in Greenland, where they were required to indicate the boundaries of the land they claimed.[31]

We left Thorfinn Karlsefne's expedition at Leiv's *Budir*, East Falmouth, where they had taken the animals ashore to feed them on the green pastures there and the people had obtained plenty of delicious whalemeat. For that reason we might think that they would stay there for some time. But as Thorfinn Karlsefne could not acquire property for his 160 men at Leiv's *Budir* (Falmouth), he had to go farther south to find a harbor with sufficient farmland for them. The saga says that the land became *vágskorið* (indented with small bays) once they left Falmouth, after they had passed *Furdustrandir*. West of Falmouth the nearest fjords are around Newport R. I. They took the ship into a *vág* (small narow bay). There they put ashore two Scots in order to let them explore the coast toward the south. Karlsefne ordered the Scots to return there in three days. This suggests that Karlsefne, with small boats, spent three days exploring the fjords around Newport to decide whether they should continue south along the coast to find a better place for settlement. When the Scots came back, one had a cluster of grapes and the other had an ear of wild wheat as proof that the land was fruitful. The saga tells that Karlsefne took the Scots aboard the ship and they left the fjord (around Newport),[32] and sailed onward on their course.

[31] Cf. Tornöe, *Lysstreif,* pp. 167-70, and cf. also *Norges Gamle Love: Frostatingsloven* XIII, 14 (N. G. L. p. 244) and *Magnus Lagaböters Landslov* VII ,19 (N. G. L. p. 116), Logfestu.

[32] In 1930 the Danish scholar Aage Roussell excavated the farm 'Sandnes' in Greenland and found there a lump of anthracite coal

This means that they continued onward in a southerly direction along the coast which the two Scottish runners had explored. Following this the saga says, '*þeir siglðu inn á fjord einn, þar lá ein ey fyri utan*', which means, 'They sailed into a fjord; there was an island outside [Block Island]'.[33] Then comes the note 19, B and N, with the following: '*þar til er vard fjardskorið; þeir logdu skipunum inn a fjordinn*'; in variant M, we find 'They sailed into a fjord, since the land was indented by fjords', and '*þarum voru straumar miklir*' which means, 'In that neighborhood were large or long streams'. Then the variant B has the note 20: '*Ok voru þar straumar miklar ok um eyna*'. That

---

(*footnote 32 cont.*)

of the same type which exists in Rhode Island. This type of coal has yet not been found in Greenland, according to Helge Ingstad. The lump of coal was found while excavating the living-room floor on the Sandnes farm. (See *Medd, om Grönland* 88, pp. 34-35.)

It seems likely that Thorfinn Karlsefne brought this lump of coal to Greenland as a souvenir from his exploration of the Rhode Island fjords.

(See *U. S. Geological Survey* 1915. Bulletin 615. Map of the Rhode Island Coal Field.)

According to the map there are coal fields all over the state of Rhode Island. In several places the coal fields are found close to the sea-level. West of Newport on 71° 20′ and 41° 31′, the coal mine seems to be close to the tidewater. On the west side of Narragansett Bay coal exists extensively. Coal is also common around Warwick, Warren, Bristol and Portsmouth.

[33] Here we have another significant statement identifying Block Island, the only island on this part of the coast situated outside a fjord. Block Island is used in the narrative as a landmark or a sailing mark for seafarers who wanted to sail into Long Island Sound, to New York Harbor (*Straumsey*).

The information about the island's *location* is much more useful to a seafarer than a name could be. When the Norsemen came from Leiv's *Budir* (Falmouth) or from Rhode Island and they discovered the island outside the fjord, then there could be no doubt about their position. If they sailed into the fjord they could not miss *Straumsey* (Manhattan). Block Island is here used as a landmark just as 'the island north of the land' (Scatari) was used as a landmark for the north coast of Vineland.

is, there were large or long streams also around the island. For that reason they called the island *Straumey* (Streams Island). The variants B, M and N have *Straumsey*.[34]

Of importance here is the fact that they sailed on a course southward from Rhode Island along the coast, and this led them into a fjord outside of which an island was located. They came from Leiv's *Budir,* south of Cape Cod, and Newport R. I. The island which lay outside the fjord must have been the sailing mark, Block Island, and the fjord must have been Long Island Sound. They sailed far into the fjords to where the land was indented with some inlets, and there were large streams. The Norse word *straum* can mean a current in the water and it can mean a sound through which a current flows. The saga writer used the plural form of the word *straum* (stream or sound). But it would not be natural to use this form for a current in the water; neither would the men of yore have used the word *mikil* (large) in connection with a current in the water. The word *sterk* (strong) would be the appropriate adjective in such instances.

At this juncture I will point to an example of how the saga of Thorfinn Karlsefne has been mistranslated and misunderstood. For this I refer to *Grönlands Historiske Mindesmærker,* Volume I, pages 412-13. As may be seen, there exist differences in various handwritten accounts concerning the fjord into which they sailed. Professor C. C. Rafn, who translated this saga from Icelandic into Danish, has done particularly good work, but it seems that here he has failed to understand the fact that *'straumar' meant sounds and not the currents in the water.*

Straumar miklar as used in the Icelandic text can hardly mean the current in the water. *Straumar miklar* can only mean long and narrow sounds, or streams like East River and Harlem River, or Kill van Kull and Staten Island Sound. Since Professor Rafn, more than a hundred years ago, translated *Straumar miklar* as strong currents (in the

[34] Concerning this see *Grönlands Historiske Mindesmærker.* Vol. I, pp. 412-13.

water), everybody, including Mr. Pohl and Mr. Holand, has written about the strong current around the island. But strong, swift currents are to be found almost everywhere along the coast. And the swiftness of the current increases and decreases from time to time. Therefore 'strong currents' does not tell us anything. Islands with strong currents around them can be found in several places in the Gulf of St. Lawrence, or in Maine. Block Island, too, answers to the description; thus the expression 'strong currents' might be taken as evidence that Karlscfne had stayed in any of these places.

But *Straumar miklar,* translated correctly as *long sounds* (long streams) around the island, tells us something. The saga about Thorfinn Karlsefne's expedition very likely referred to the long, narrow sound around Manhattan in New York Harbor. Currents of water encircle every island, but Manhattan has these long narrow sounds or streams around it. The name they gave to the place, *Straumsey* (Streams Island) was apt. There is, indeed, strong evidence in favor of identifying *Straumsey* with Manhattan, but this evidence has not hitherto been accepted by any historian.

The word *mikil* means big or large. One does not talk about a large current in the water, but of a strong current. However, one can use *mikil* to refer to a long sound or a stream flowing through a sound. And the saga uses the plural form of the word for sound, i.e., *Straumar.* Thus it is very plain that the writer of those times must have had in mind several sounds (or narrow passages of water between two lands, two islands, etc.), through which streams or currents flowed. In Norway there are many examples of such sounds along the coast, and they are indicated by the word *Straum.* The best known of these are the *Saltstraum* and the *Moskenesstraum.*

There were long or large streams flowing around the island. Thus they called that island *Straumsey.* It seems very possible that Karlsefne's *Straumsey* is identical with our Manhattan Island. As one comes sailing through Long

Island Sound one may continue either north around Manhattan or south around it. Therefore, one can say that the streams flow *around* the island, which is why they named it *Straumsey*. But the fjord into which those long streams flowed they called *Straumsfjord* (Streams-fjord). Their *Straumsfjord* can hardly be anything but the modern New York Harbor, running clear out to Sandy Hook and into Hudson River (see below).

Long Island Sound has the appearance of a fjord, but it does not terminate, as a fjord must, and is in fact a sound leading into New York Harbor. But we can easily understand why the saga writer used the word 'fjord' for it, since only the East River separates the Bronx from Queens, and Long Island from Manhattan. The saga therefore rings true in its description of how as they sailed in through Long Island Sound, the land became indented with several inlets (i.e., *vágskorið*). Several such inlets are found both on Long Island and on the Mainland (Queens and Bronx). The account in the saga corresponds very well with the area covered by the modern New York City.

The area of New York Harbor is remarkable for its many sounds (*straumar*). First, we have the one flowing from Long Island Sound to Manhattan; and this, in turn, is divided into two branch streams, namely Harlem River and East River, though the saga seems to indicate that they thought of it as one stream around Manhattan. Another typical stream or *straum* is Kill van Kull, leading into Newark Bay. In addition we have Staten Island Sound between Staten Island and New Jersey. This is also a typical *straum* (stream). And these streams are longer than most streams in Norway and Greenland. Thus the men of that time could hardly think of a more appropriate name for New York Harbor than *Straumsfjord*.

Manhattan was at that time, as now, the most centrally located point on the American east coast. From Manhattan, with their ships and boats, they could roam as far as they wished over an extensive area. There were means of communication in almost every direction. By following the

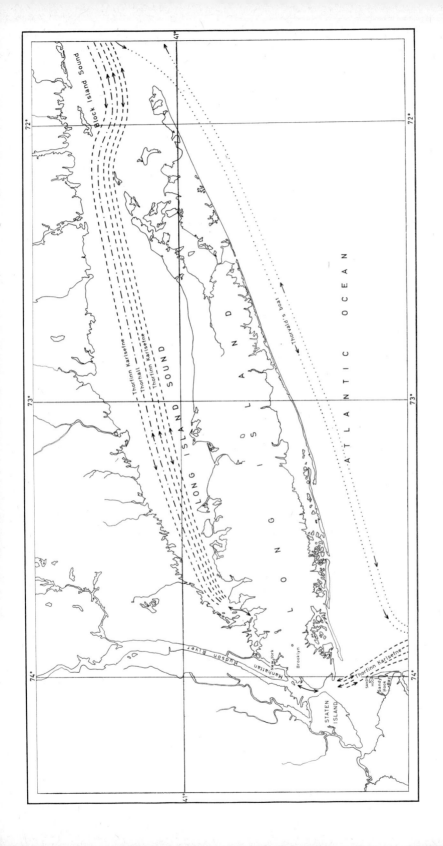

Hudson River they could reach wide fields for hunting purposes on both sides of the river. Along the so-called streams they obtained access to large areas of New Jersey; and along Long Island Sound they found important regions for both hunting and fishing. Nor was it far to the Lower Bay, for fishing purposes. And both Long Island and Staten Island could be advantageously utilized in various ways. From Manhattan and the smaller islands the wild animals could be eradicated and the place made safe for their domestic animals. Enough lumber was available for their various purposes, and there was a sufficiency of good soil for the production of the grain, flax, and hemp they needed.

But the East River was of particular importance as a protected harbor for the ships and boats of that time. The quality of this harbor would be sufficient reason for them to return there no matter where they otherwise journeyed. As good a base as the East River for exploratory trips to places near and far is not found anywhere else on the coast. There their ships could lie at anchor safely even under the severe weather conditions that could arise from time to time.

To Karlsefne, approaching from the north and now searching for a well-protected and central harbor for his large expedition, Long Island Sound had the appearance of a fjord with the desired advantages. They sailed so far in, according to the saga, that they reached the stretch where the land is indented with inlets, which indicates that they had passed into East River, between the Bronx and Queens. They had come to the head of the 'fjord', where the inlets afforded good harbors, and the expedition could settle down for a period of rest.

It may well be imagined that reconnaissance parties in small boats were sent onward to the southernmost point of Manhattan to explore mooring possibilities. The party would soon observe that the Hudson River would not provide a good haven in gales from the north or the south. A trip over to Staten Island and along the southwestern shore of Brooklyn would have shown them that there

104

existed no harbor and landing place that would be suitable in *all* kinds of weather. Thus the party could report that the best headquarters for the expedition was undoubtedly East River, where they had an ideal base for the ships in any sort of weather.

They unloaded their cargo and made preparations to remain there — such as clearing the ground and building houses. And they found pastures for the domestic animals which they had brought with them. In this connection the saga variants B, M, and N, say: '*Ok leitudu ser þar land-snytja. Fjoll voru þar, ok fagert var þar um at litast.*' That is, 'they utilized the land. There were mountains and the land was wonderful to look at.' The grass was very high, but they devoted nearly all their time to exploration and stayed there during the winter, which was a severe one, without having gathered fodder in the summer, having come there too late in the year, one supposes, to sow any grain. During the next summer there was less in the way of successful hunting and fishing, and it became difficult to provide enough food for the people.[35]

Here we have another fact that suggests that *Straumsey* was Manhattan. The winter on Manhattan is always severe, due to the masses of cold water that the Hudson River brings down to New York Harbor. Almost every winter the waters around Manhattan are frozen, even with the heavy traffic of all kinds of ships in the harbor. Sometimes the ice can reach all the way over to Staten Island. On the 12th of January, 1959, I had the opportunity to see the ferry sailing through broken ice all the way from Manhattan to Staten Island.

It may be that the ice around Manhattan in a severe winter could have prevented Karlsefne's men from going out fishing. This could possibly be one of the reasons for lack of food, as well as for Karlsefne's going farther south to *Hop* for the next winter. No island other than Man-

[35] See *Grönlands Historiske Mindesmærker,* V. I. p. 414. 'They stayed there on Manhattan over the winter, and the winter was severe.'

hattan is frozen up so far south on the American coast. In my opinion Manhattan is the only island on this part of the coast where the Norsemen would say that the winter was severe. This, too, indicates that Manhattan was the island where Thorfinn Karlsefne's expedition lived during their first winter in America.

Later on the weather improved, making it possible for them to do more extensive fishing. The variants B, M, and N, say: '*Um várid fara þeir inn i Straumsfjorð, ok hofdu fong af hvorutveggja landinu, veidar af meginlandinu, eggvar* (on the island), *ok utrodra af sjonum.*' That is, 'In the spring they went into *Straumsfjord* [from Manhattan into Hudson River], and they hunted with good results on both lands [both sides of the river] — hunting on the *mainland,* gathering eggs on the island, and fishing in the sea.'

The above is a most interesting piece of information. From this we can easily surmise, as mentioned earlier, that their *Straumsfjord* is identical with New York Harbor going into Hudson River.

If their *Straumsfjord* had been Long Island Sound, they could not have said *into Straumsfjord.* They would have had to say *out of Straumsfjord,* since Long Island Sound extends from Manhattan out into the main ocean. Thus they were under the impression that *Straumsfjord* reached farther in than to Manhattan Island, as they had to go farther into the fjord to the mainland. *Straumsfjord* therefore blends in with the Hudson River. It is somewhat difficult to determine the line of demarcation between the fjord and the river; but it would not be illogical to assume that they calculated the fjord to reach as far to the north as to Bear Mountain. It is always customary to say *into* or *out of* a fjord, no matter what the direction of the fjord might be. *Out of* means from the head to the mouth of such a long body of water, and *into* means the reverse. That they went up to the *mainland* for hunting shows that these Norsemen resided on an *island,* and that must have been Manhattan. Thorhall also took water on his ship as it lay at an island, according to the saga.

Henry Collins Brown [36] says about Manhattan:

'A fresh-water lake, deep enough to float an ocean liner, lay in the middle of the island, between Worth and Duane Streets and from the Bowery to Broadway and is now covered by the Country Court Buildings and new Civic Center. Rippling streams and gurgling springs flowed everywhere.'

Manhattan — *Manhado* — means Island of the Hills (Indian). It is 12.5 miles long, 2.5 miles wide, and its highest point is 268 feet. On the northern part of it are some stony hills above the Harlem River. It may well be that it was just here that Karlsefne and Bjarne found Thorhall Veidemann after searching for him for three days. They found him on *'hamargnipu einni'*. *Hamar* (cliff) is exactly the word in the Icelandic language that would be used about this hill. There is no such *hamar* on Staten Island or Long Island. The word *hamar* indicates Northern Manhattan, as the only place on an island on this part of the coast where such features are to be found.

The lake in the middle of the island north of City Hall must have been of the greatest value to the Norse settlers. There the water supply was secured for the summer as well as for the winter time. We can well understand that this lake was the natural center of their activities on Manhattan (*Straumsey*) and that they had to build their first houses near the river that flowed from the lake. Later on it is likely that they could secure some water supply in the area of Central Park and several other places where they took land for their farms. But the water supply was so important that we can be sure that they built their homes where there was an opportunity to have fresh running water near the houses.

It is also obvious that they were dependent on fishing for obtaining food from day to day; and it appears probable that they could fish in Long Island Sound with considerably better results than in the Lower Bay (of *Straumsfjord*), bordering on the open ocean. At that time salt for the

[36] *The Story of Old New York,* p. 26.

preservation of fish and meat could be produced only by boiling sea-water which made it rather scarce and expensive. Thus, fish and meat were dried for storage purposes. But in the fall it would be difficult, in that mild and damp climate, to keep these products sufficiently dry to prevent them from becoming spoiled. No doubt they were quite dependent on fresh supplies of meat and fish. Accordingly Manhattan remained the permanent center for their hunting and fishing expeditions.

When Thorhall Veidemann prepared to leave Vineland, he did so in the harbor *by the island* (Manhattan). It is evident from the old record that he became quite disappointed with the prospects in America. He had been promised wine to drink, he said, but he had obtained only water. In addition even simple food was scarce at times. Therefore, he found it preferable to return to Greenland. But Karlsefne wished to move farther south in order to explore the land more thoroughly. Only nine men departed with Thorhall; and it was told later how they had drifted across the Atlantic to Ireland, where they were captured and made slaves. The rest of the 160 men remained with Karlsefne.

It is told in the saga that Snorre was the first white man known for certain to have been born in Vineland (America). He was three years old when they departed from *Straumsey* (Manhattan) and returned to Greenland. It seems, therefore, that they intended to establish a permanent Norse settlement in America. It is probable that they built durable houses and took other measures necessary for the foundation of a permanent colony.

After the first winter on Manhattan the saga reveals that Thorfinn Karlsefne intended to explore the land further to the south in order to find a more convenient base for the next winter's expedition. If we think of a winter like that of 1960-61, when about 70 inches of snow fell in Manhattan, we can well understand Karlsefne's intention to move farther south for the next winter. We assume that some of the men from Thorvald's expedition who had seen the American coast to the south were with Karlsefne. They probably recommended an exploration of Delaware Bay and Chesapeake Bay, with Delaware Bay as their first objective.

They would have found in Delaware Bay a fruitful region for exploration; they very likely went up the river a good distance in their smaller boats. We may even assume that they had constructed river craft especially suitable for the purpose. Even though they went far up the river, however, they would not be occupied for the entire summer; they would most likely have sufficient time for a trip to Chesapeake Bay to examine that region. Karlsefne would not have been satisfied with anything less.

It is said that they sailed for a long time along the coast, so the voyage could not have been a mere transfer over a short distance from *Straumsey*. Nor would they move to a place with less available space and fewer advantages. They naturally sought larger and richer districts for their special purpose, and a better area than that around *Straumsfjord* (New York) was not to be found before they reached Chesapeake Bay. This also corresponds well with the fact that they sailed for a long time along the coast toward the south. But there exists another item of information which supports the contention that *Hop* was a place in Chesapeake Bay.

It is related that Karlsefne, after returning from *Hop* to *Straumsfjord,* went with one ship northward hoping to find Thorhall Veidemann. He passed by *Kjalarnes* (Cape Cod), where they saw uninhabited forests as far as the eye could reach, and almost no opening in the wooded areas. From there they sailed on for a long time, and then saw mountain ridges on the land. When exchanging opinions about what they had seen, they said that those mountains very probably belonged to the same mountain chain which they had seen when they were at *Hop*. They also had the idea that it was about the same distance from *Straumsfjord* to *Hop* as from *Straumsfjord* to those heights in the north where they were. Karlsefne and his men had just then traveled over both distances, one immediately after the other. They were therefore in a position to have a strong foundation for their judgment in this matter. Those mountain ridges they saw in the north must have been the heights of Maine, near Portland. Looking at the map, we see that the distance from Portland to New York (*Straumsfjord*) is about the same as the distance from New York to Norfolk (Chesapeake Bay). They had seen the same mountains while traveling up the Hudson River, Delaware River, Susquehanna River and the Potomac River during their four years in America. In Europe at that time travelers were accustomed to following the river courses. The Norsemen journeyed with their ships on the Russian rivers from the Baltic Sea to the Black and Caspian Seas, a most natural thing to do in that day and age. The Norsemen resided at *Hop* during the winter, and no snow fell there. This also indicates that they were as far south as Chesapeake Bay. Their domestic animals were also pastured throughout the winter.

When they arrived in Chesapeake Bay, they would soon discover that this region offered them many more advantages than were apparent along Delaware Bay. Chesapeake Bay is an enormous enclosed complex of fjords, ideal for the boats and ships used by the Norsemen. There it was possible for them to move around extensively on the fjords and the large rivers; and everywhere they could find the best kind of natural harbors for their vessels. It was a territory fully as good as *Straumsfjord* and *Straumsey*. They did not need to travel any further in order to find enough space for their entire expedition. As their central place of settlement they established a site which they called *Hop*. This name indicates especially a small enclosed harbor. In this case, it was a lagoon in a little river. The name *Hop* is appropriate for a lagoon. The river was so shallow that their vessels could not float into the lagoon at low tide. In some old saga versions, it is said that the tide had to rise at least halfway before their ships could move into the lagoon. There they had a good natural harbor.

110

There exist two accounts of Karlsefne's journey to *Hop*. One says that Karlsefne, Snorre, and Bjarne traveled far to the south along the coast until they arived at the place they called *Hop* with the entire crew and all their domestic animals! The saga variants K and M state, 'There are also some people who say that at first, only Karlsefni, Snori, and 40 men went southward with one ship. But Bjarni and Gudrid remained at *Straumsey* with 100 men [*Xtigir* men]. Karlsefne and Snorre stayed at *Hop* only two months. Then they returned to *Straumsey* and fetched the people remaining there, after which they resided at *Hop* during the ensuing winter.'

This second and more detailed account is the more informative, and it undoubtedly gives us the correct picture of what happened. Karlsefne, Snorre and forty men first made an exploratory journey. They found *Hop* and built houses for the people and then went back to *Straumsey* and fetched the rest of the expedition.

The difference is only that some of the variants of the saga leave out the narrative about Karlsefne's and Snorre's exploratory journey to *Hop,* and tell only about their last journey from *Straumsey* to *Hop* to bring the people and the cattle.

We know that the people of *Straumsey* were short of food the first spring. For that reason they had to stay at *Straumsey* till they had harvested the first crops of barley, rye and wheat, which were to form their basic food supply for the next winter and summer.

It would have been disastrous to take the whole expedition aboard the ships and start to search for another place to live before they had sufficient food, which they would not have until the next harvest. But it made sense for Karlsefne, Snorre and forty men to explore southward in the summertime. They chose *Hop,* and built the houses there in the summer; with the crop from *Straumsey* their food supply was secured till they harvested another crop in *Hop*. But we can be sure that some of the party remained in *Straumsey* in order to take care of the houses, and to sow

grain for the next summer. The saga says that when the
expedition returned from *Hop* a year or two later, they had
plenty of everything in *Straumsey,* which indicates that
some of the men remained there and did not go to *Hop.*
Karlsefne had some of his men in Falmouth, some in Manhattan, and the rest of his party in Chesapeake Bay.

Where was Hop?

Thorfinn Karlsefne sailed for a long time till he came to
a river which flowed down from the country and passed
through a lake out to sea. This could not be a small river,
but would have to be one of the major rivers that flow into
Chesapeake Bay. A general survey indicates the Patuxent
as the river which runs through a lake out to the sea.
When one approaches from the sea, the course of the
Patuxent is only visible for some two miles west of Drum
Point as far as Point Patience, where the river suddenly
changes its direction to the northwest and broadens into a
lake. There were great shoals (*eyrar*) so that they could not
enter the river except at high tide. Some variants have half
tide. This seems to fit the Patuxent, and some writers have
thought this inner pool to be the lake which Karlsefne
named *Hop.* But then on the north side of the Patuxent
estuary is Fresh Creek, which could very well have been
the little lake which Karlsefne chose as a harbor for the
ships and named *Hop.*

There were, in my opinion, several good reasons why
they should have chosen Fresh Creek as a harbor. On the
east side of Chesapeake Bay there are some islands where
there certainly were seals and birds at that time. The seal
was an important animal in the Greenlander's household
because it yielded fat for light and several other purposes;
furthermore, the skin was good for clothing and the meat
was excellent food. The distance from Fresh Creek to the
islands was great enough to prevent their presence from
disturbing the seals. From Fresh Creek it was also easy
to row out for fishing. They even made pits in the sand

and when the tide ebbed fish were trapped in the pits.

For hunting they could sail inland on the Patuxent. Nor was it far to the Potomac River, another good waterway to

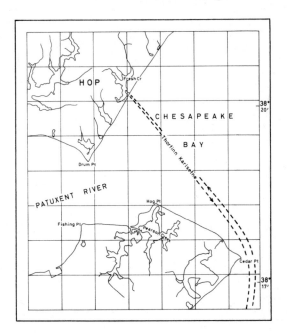

the interior. Fresh Creek was centrally located in the middle of Chesapeake Bay.

The fresh water protected their ships against the wood-eating teredos as well as barnacles, and it was a safe harbor in all kinds of weather.

In *Hop* they found wild wheat (wild rice?) wherever the ground was low, and vines on the hills (*holt*). *Holt* means small wooded hills. This is important information for locating *Hop,* as in the areas north of the Patuxent River there are small wooded hills, which are not found in Delaware Bay or in the southern part of Chesapeake Bay.

When the Indians visited *Hop,* they came from the south and passed a *nes* (point). I propose that the *nes* was Cedar Point, which can be seen from Fresh Creek, but not from

113

a harbor further up or west in the river. The Indians also withdrew to the south and would disappear south of Cedar Point.

Karlsefne's defense plan

The *Flateyarbok,* Chapter 5, also has a description fitting Fresh Creek as the place where the Norsemen lived.

' "Nú munum vèr þurfa til ráða at taka", segir Karlsefni, "þviat ek hygg at þeir muni vitja vor hitt priðja sinni með ufriði ok fjölmenni. Nú skulum vèr taka þat rað, at X menn fari fram á nes þetta, ok sýni sic þar; en annat lið vort skal fara i skóg, ok höggva þar rjóðr fyrir nautfé vort, þá er liðit kemer fram or skóginum. Vèr skulum ok taka griðúng vorn, ok láta hann fara fyrir oss." En þar var svâ háttat, er fundr þeira var ætlaðr, at vatn var öðrumegin, en skógr á annan veg. Nu veru þessi ráð höfð, er Karlsefni lagði til. Nú komu Skrælingjar i þann stað, er Karlsefni hafði ætlat til bardaga; nú varð þar bardagi, ok fèll fjöldi af liði krælingja.'

[' "Now it will be necessary to make a good defense plan," said Karlsefne, "as I assume that many more will come back for the third time and bring war upon us. We should decide to let ten men operate on the *nes* [point] to attract the attention of the Skrelings. But the rest of our men should go to the wood and cut a way for our cattle in case the Skrelings attack through the wood. We should also let our bull go in front of us." The battlefield had a lake on one side and the wood on the other side. Karlsefne's defense plan was now accepted. The Skrelings came to the battlefield Karlsefne had chosen; they fought and many of the Skrelings fell there.']

When studying the map in order to see if Karlsefne's plan tallies with the area around Fresh Creek, the first feature we search for is the *nes* (point) which Karlsefne mentioned. We see that a point extends from the north shore of Fresh Creek into the lake. The battlefield could extend from this *nes* to the northeast, with the lake to the east and the wood to the west. That fits exactly the description given in the saga.

114

The houses were situated on the northwest side of the lake (*ovanfor vatnet*), some near the lake and some more distant. If the Indians were not peaceful, they would probably steal weapons, food and goods, or even damage the houses. Karlsefne planned to prevent the Indians from doing any harm to his party. He ordered ten men to create a diversion on the *nes* in the hope that the Indians would concentrate their attack there. It is probable that he had reinforcements ready to join the ten and form a line of battle across the *nes* from shore to shore. If the enemy were not too numerous he could then contain them and drive them back to their canoes. But if the Norsemen were forced to retire they had to take the greatest care to avoid encirclement. The terrain behind the Norsemen was higher, so that the Indians would always have to attack uphill if the Norsemen retired. This was to the advantage of the Norsemen, who most likely kept their left flank to the water, while their right flank would fall further back into the wood. In order to prevent the Indians from encircling their right flank, Karlsefne ordered his men to cut an opening in the wood for their cattle, where he planned to retire the right flank. There the cattle would be able to protect Karlsefne's right wing; he and his men had previously noticed that the Indians were afraid of their cattle.

The *Flateyarbok*, Chapter 5, reveals:

'After the first winter came the summer; then they became aware of the Indians; and a great flock of men came out of the wood. Their cattle were just there and a bull started to bellow very loudly. That scared the Indians, who ran away with their burdens.'

The version in the *Hauksbok* runs:

'It happened that a bull belonging to Karlsefni's party ran out of the woods, and bellowed loudly; this terrified the savages, and they ran out to their canoes, and rowed south along the coast. . .'

But the Indians came back later in greater numbers, and it was for this event that Karlsefne had made his defense plans. When the struggle started, the Norsemen were scared by a 'globe' which the Skrelings threw. The Norsemen also had the impression that the Indians attacked not only from the canoes at the point, but also from the woods. This attack against their right flank made the Norsemen afraid of being surrounded by the Indians, and they withdrew or fled to some rocks or hills further up along the river. This is probably the river coming from the northeast into Fresh Creek. If they thought that the Indians were attacking from the southwest through the woods, it would be natural for the Norsemen to retreat along this river. But after the battle they discovered that the attack from the woods was a feint (*Synkverving*).

The saga provides further support for Fresh Creek as the location of *Hop*. The hills it mentions (p. 88) signify the almost untranslatable Icelandic words *holt* and *loegdir,* indicating an undulating terrain — alternating long low ridges and valleys. According to the saga Karlsefne's men found vines growing on the ridges, and grain in the valleys. Land fitting this description can be found north and west of Chesapeake Bay, well within reach of Karlsefne's men.

Karlsefne's dispositions along the American coast

It is revealed in the *Flateyarbok* that Karlsefne had 60 men and five women on his ship. If the two other ships had 50 men each, then there would be 160 men, as stated in the *Hauksbok*.

The *Hauksbok* reveals that some people 'say that at first, only Karlsefni, Snori and 40 men went southward with one ship. But Bjarni and Gudrid remained at *Straumsey* with 100 men' (*Xtigir* men). This means 140 men, but there were 160 men altogether. Even though eight men went along with Thorhall, we still have 10-12 men to account for. These men were probably left in Falmouth to take care of Leiv Eiriksson's houses. Food production was the most

116

important task in the years of the expedition, and it was even more important if more settlers should decide to come from Greenland. Therefore it is likely that the party in Falmouth had to catch and dry codfish during the winter and produce grain in the summer. We must consider this to be a preliminary expedition, planned to last for 3-4 years, since there were 160 men and only five women. They would certainly not attempt to establish a permanent colony with only five women. We must assume that most of the 160 men were married and wanted to take their families to America when they had prepared a homestead, built houses, and stored some food.

In order to select homesteads, they had to survey the land, which explains their exploration of the American rivers up to the mountains. We can recall the mountain chain that they believed to extend from Maine to *Hop*. This cannot be fiction. They knew that the mountains were there. They had seen parts of them from the rivers. Thorfinn Karlsefne's expedition had, in the course of three to four years, gained a good knowledge of America from Nova Scotia to Chesapeake Bay. When Thorfinn Karlsefne came to America, he landed first at Cape Cod, where Thorvald had raised the keel of his ship as a sailing mark. Karlsefne continued to Falmouth where he stopped for some time. Afterward he investigated the fjords of Rhode Island, and continued past Block Island via Long Island Sound to Manhattan, where he remained for a year. From Manhattan he and forty of his men explored the land down to Chesapeake Bay, where he chose *Hop* as the new settlement for the expedition. In the autumn he sailed back from *Hop* to *Straumsey* (Manhattan) and fetched the rest of his party; and then Karlsefne sailed to *Hop* for the second time. When he left *Hop*, Karlsefne sailed for the fourth time along the coast from Chesapeake Bay to New York. And then he sailed with one ship in search of Thorhall Veidemann, past Cape Cod to Maine and probably to Nova Scotia. He sailed back to Manhattan where he remained with the expedition till the next summer, when it sailed back to Greenland.

117

Karlsefne and his crew had sailed four times along the coast from Nova Scotia to New York and must have become quite familiar with this littoral region of America. By now, hundreds of Greenlanders and Icelanders had visited America, but at that time it was not customary to make records of such adventures in writing. Nevertheless they have left us the record of the Vineland voyages. We know, too, that Greenlanders and Icelanders traveled all over Europe at that time, and so spread their knowledge of America.

Bibliography

Ahlenius, Karl: *Olaus Magnus och hans framställning af Nordens geografi*. Uppsala 1895

Andersen, Magnus: *Vikingefærden*. Kristiania 1895

Anderson, Rasmus B.: *America not Discovered by Columbus*. Chicago 1874

Babcock, William H.: *Early Norse Visits to North America*. Smithsonian Miscellaneous Collections, Vol. 59 No. 19, Washington 1913

— Recent History and Present Status of the Vinland Problem. *Geographical Review*, Vol. 11, New York 1921, pp. 265-82

Bancroft, George: *History of the United States, from the discovery of the American continent to the present time*. Vol. 1, Boston 1834, 4th ed. 1838

Bang, Anton: *History of the United States*. Christiania 1863

Bárðarson, Ivar: *Det gamle Grönlands Beskrivelse*. Published from manuscript of Finnur Jónsson, Copenhagen 1930

Beamish, North Ludlow: *The Discovery of America by the Northmen*. Boston 1841

Berg, Henry: Vinland og Tidevannet. *Årbok* for 1955, Det Kongelige Norske Videnskabers Selskab Museet, Trondhjem 1956, pp. 45-65

Björnbo, Axel Anthon: *Adam af Bremens Nordensopfattelse*. Copenhagen 1910

— *Cartographia Groenlandica*. Meddelelser om Grönland, Vol. 48, Copenhagen 1911-12

Bobé Louis: Aktstykker til Oplysning om Grönlands Besejling 1521-1607, *Danske Magazin*, Ser. 5 Vol. 6, Copenhagen 1909, pp. 303-11

Bolton, Charles Knowles: *Terra Nova: the northeast coast of America before 1602*. Boston 1935

Brenner, Oscar: *Die ächte Karte des Olaus Magnus vom Jahre 1539 nach dem Exemplar der Münchener Staatsbibliotek*. Videnskabsselskabets Forhandlinger No. 15, Christiania 1886

Brögger, Anton Wilhelm: *Gamle Emigranter.* Oslo 1928
— *Ancient Emigrants.* Oxford 1929
— *Den norske bosetningen på Shetland, Orkenöyene.* Det norske Videnskaps-Akademis Skrifter, Hist. Filos. Kl. 1930, No. 3, Oslo 1930
— Den norske bosetningen på Færöyene. *Norsk Geografisk Tidsskrift,* Vol. 5 No. 6, Oslo 1935, pp. 321-33
— *Vinlandsferdene.* Oslo 1937

Bröndsted, Johannes: *Norsemen in North America before Columbus.* Copenhagen 1951

Brunn, Daniel: *Eirik den Röde.* Copenhagen 1915

Bugge, Alexander: Vore forfædres opdagelsesreiser i polaregnene. *Kringsjaa,* Vol. 11, Kristiania 1898, pp. 497-509
— Spörsmaalet om Vinland. *Maal og Minne,* Kristiania 1911, pp. 226-36
— Skibsfarten fra de ældste tider til omkring aar 1600. *Den Norske Sjöfarts Historie,* Vol. 1, Kristiania 1923, pp. 7-369

Bugge, Sophus: Hönen-Runerne fra Ringerike. *Norges Indskrifter med de yngre Runer,* Kristiania 1902

Daae, Ludvig: Didrik Pining. *Historisk Tidsskrift,* Ser. 2 Vol. 3, Kristiania 1882, pp. 233-45
— Mere om Didrik Pining. *Historisk Tidsskrift,* Ser. 3 Vol. 4, Kristiania 1898, pp. 195-97

DeCosta, Benjamin Franklin: *Notes of the Pre-Columbian discovery of America by the Northmen.* Charlestown 1869
— *The Pre-Columbian discovery of America by the Northmen with translations from the Icelandic sagas.* 2nd ed., Albany 1890

Delabarre, Edmund Burke: *Dighton Rock: A Study of the Written Rocks of New England.* New York 1928

DeRoo, P.: *History of America before Columbus, according to documents and approved authors.* Philadelphia 1900

Dieserud, Juul: Norse Discoveries in America. *Bulletin of the American Geographical Society,* Vol. 33 No. 1, New York 1901, pp. 1-18

Duff, Charles: *The Truth about Columbus.* London 1957

Espeland, Anton: Sjöfareren Didrik Pining. Norsk admiral, opdagelsesreisende og kaperförer. *Norges Sjöforsvar,* Årgang 2 No. 3, Oslo 1932, pp. 49-53

Falk, Hjalmar: *Altwestnordische Kleiderkunde mit besonderer Berücksichtigung der Terminologie.* Videnskabsselskabets Skrifter, Hist. Filos. Kl. 1918, No. 3, Kristiania 1919

Fernald, Merritt Lyndon: Notes on the plants of Wineland the Good. *Rhodora, Journal of the New England Botanical Club,* Vol. 12, Boston 1910

Fernald, Merritt Lyndon: The natural history of Ancient Vinland and its geographical significance. *Bulletin of the American Geographical Society*, Vol. 47 No. 9, New York 1915, pp. 686-87

Fischer, Josef: *Die Entdeckungen der Normannen in Amerika*. Freiburg i. Br. 1902, English ed. 1903

Fiske, John: *The Discovery of America*, Vols I-II. London 1892
— *Old Virginia and her neighbours*. Boston and New York 1897

Forster, J. Reinhold: *Geschichte der Entdeckungen und Schiffahrten im Norten*. Frankfurt 1784

Fossum, Andrew: *The Norse discovery of America*. Minneapolis 1918

Gathorne-Hardy, Geoffrey Malcolm: *The Norse Discoverers of America. The Wineland Sagas translated and discussed*. Oxford 1921
— A Recent Journey to Northern Labrador. *The Geographical Journal*, Vol. 59 No. 3, London 1922 pp. 153-67

Gebhardi, L. A.: *Kongeriget Norges historie*, Vols. I-II. Odense 1777-78

Geelmuyden, H.: Om gamle Kalendere, særlig Islændernes. *Naturen*, Aargang 7 No. 3, Kristiania 1883, pp. 37-43

Gini, Corrado: De norröne grönlandsbygders undergang. *Naturen*, årgang 81 No. 7, Bergen 1957, pp. 410-32

Gjerset, Knut: *History of the Norwegian People*. Vols. I-II, New York 1915, two vols. in one, New York 1927

Gosling, W. G.: *Labrador: its discovery, exploration and development*. London 1910

Gray, Edward F.: *Leiv Eriksson, discoverer of America, A. D. 1003*. London 1930

Greenland, Vols. I-III. Commission for the direction of the geological and geographical investigations in Greenland, Copenhagen 1928-29

Grönlands Historiske Mindesmærker, Vols. I-III. Copenhagen 1838-45

Harrisse, Henry: *The discovery of North America*. London and Paris 1892
— *John Cabot, the discoverer of North America, and Sebastian his son*. London 1896

Haskins, Charles Homer: *The Renaissance of the Twelfth Century*. Cambridge 1928

Haugen, Einar: *Voyages to Vinland. The First American Saga*. New York 1942

Hermansson, Halldór: The Vinland voyages: A few suggestions. *Geographical Review*, Vol. 17 No. 1, New York 1927, pp. 107-14
— *The problem of Wineland*. Islandica, Vol. 25. Ithaca 1936

Herteig, Asbjörn E.: The excavation of 'Bryggen', the old Hanseatic Wharf in Bergen. *Medieval Archeology* Vol. III, 1959, pp. 177-86

Hertzberg, Ebbe: Nordboernes gamle Boldspil. *Historiske Skrifter* dedicated to Prof. Ludvig Daae on his 70th birthday, Dec. 7, Christiania 1904

Holand, Hjalmar R.: *The Kensington Stone. A Study in Pre-Columbian American History.* Ephraim 1932
— The 'Myth' of the Kensington Stone. *New England Quarterly,* Vol. 8, 1935, pp. 42-62
— *Westward from Vineland.* New York 1940
— *America 1355-1364.* New York 1946
— *Explorations in America before Columbus.* New York 1956
— *A Pre-Columbian Crusade to America.* New York 1962

Holm, Gustav: *Small additions to the Vinland problem.* Meddelelser om Grönland, Vol. 59, Copenhagen 1924

Holtved, Erik: Har nordboerne vært i Thule distriktet? *Fra Nationalmuseets Arbejdsmark,* Copenhagen 1945, pp. 79-84

Horsford, Eben Norton: *The problem of the Northmen.* A letter to Judge Daly, the President of the American Geographical Society. Cambridge 1889
— *The landfall of Leiv Erikson, A. D. 1000 and the site of his houses in Vineland.* Boston 1892
— *Discovery of America by Northmen.* (Address at the unveiling of the statue of Leiv Eriksen delivered Oct. 29, 1887) Boston and New York 1888

Hovgaard, William: *The Voyages of the Norsemen to America.* New York 1914

Howley, M. F.: *Vinland vindicated.* Canadian Royal Society 1898

Humboldt, Alexander von: *Kritische Untersuchungen über die historische Entwickelung der geographischen Kentnisse von der neuen Welt.* Berlin 1836-52

Ingstad, Helge: *Landet under Leidarstjernen.* Oslo 1959

Irgens, O.: *Et Spörgsmaal vedkommende de gamle Nordmænds oversöiske Fart.* Bergens Historiske Forenings Skrifter No. 10, Bergen 1904

Jameson, John Franklin: *Original Narratives of American History.* Vol. I, New York 1905 (contains also Julius E. Olson's edition of the tales of the Vineland voyages)

Johnsen, Oscar Albert: *Noregsveldets undergang.* Kristiania 1924

Jones, Gwyn: *The Norse Atlantic Saga. Being the Norse Voyages of Discovery and Settlement to Iceland, Greenland, America.* London 1964

Jónsson, Arngrim: *Gröenlandia eller Historie av Grönland.* Copenhagen 1732

Jónsson, Finnur: Erik den rödes Saga og Vinland. *Historisk Tids-skrift*, Ser. 5 Vol. I, Kristiania 1912, pp. 116-47
– Opdagelsen af og Rejserne til Vinland. *Aarböger for nordisk Old-kyndighed og Historie*. Copenhagen 1915, pp. 205-21
– *Den oldnorske og oldislandske litteraturs historie*. 2nd. ed., Copenhagen 1920-24
– Flateyjarbók. *Aarböger for nordisk Oldkyndighed og Historie*. Copenhagen 1927, pp. 139-90
– (Ari þorgilsson) *Islendingabok*. Tilegnet Islands Alting 930-1930. Dansk-Islandsk Forbundsfond, Copenhagen 1930

Kendrick, T. D.: *A History of the Vikings*. London 1930

Koht, Halvdan: The finding of America by the Norsemen. *Norwegian Trade Review*, Vol. 9 No. 3, Oslo 1926, pp. 37-43
– Review of Scisco: 'The Tradition of Hvittramanna-land' (Sag-net om Hvitramannaland). *Historisk Tidsskrift*, Ser. 4 Vol. 6, Kristiania 1910, pp. 132-36
– Norsk historieskrivning under kong Sverre, serskilt Sverre-Soga. *Edda*, Vol. 2, Kristiania 1914, pp. 67-102

Kolsrud, Oluf: Til Östgrönlands historie. *Norsk Geografisk Tidsskrift*, Vol. 5 No. 6, Oslo 1935, pp. 381-413

Kretschmer, Konrad: *Dei Entdeckung Amerikas in ihrer Bedeutung für die Geschichte des Weltbildes*. Berlin 1892

Larsen, Sofus: Danmark og Portugal i 15de Aarhundrede. *Aarböger for nordisk Oldkyndighed og Historie*. Copenhagen 1919, pp. 236-312
– *Kilderne til Olaf Trygvasons Saga*. Copenhagen 1932
– *The discovery of North America twenty years before Columbus*. Copenhagen 1924

Larson, Laurence Marcellus: The Vinland Voyages. *The American Scandinavian Review*, Vol. 11 No. 9, New York, Sept. 1923, pp. 531-47
– The Kensington Rune Stone. *Minnesota History*, Vol. 17, Minnesota Historical Society, St. Paul 1936, pp. 20-37

Loffler, E.: *The Vineland-excursions of the ancient Scandinavians*. Amerikanistkongressens forhandlinger, Copenhagen 1883
– *The Vineland Excursions of the ancient Scandinavians*. Copenhagen 1894

Magnússon, Finn: Om de Engelske Handel og Færd paa Island i det 15de Aarhundrede, især med Hensyn til Columbus's formeentlige Reise dertil i Aaret 1477, og hans Beretninger desangaaende. *Nordisk Tidsskrift for Oldkyndighed*, Vol. 2, Copenhagen 1833, pp. 112-69

Mathiassen, Therkel: *Skrælingene i Grönland. Grönlændernes Historie, belyst gjennem Udgravninger*. Copenhagen 1935

123

Merrill, William Stetson: The Vinland problem through four centuries. *The Catholic Historical Review,* Washington, April 1935

Mjelde, M. M.: Eyktarstadproblemet og Vinlandsreisene. *Historisk Tidsskrift,* Ser. 5 Vol. 6, Oslo 1927, pp. 259-81, English summary

Morison, S. E.: *Admiral of the Ocean Sea.* Boston 1942

Moulton and Yates: *History of the State of New York.* New York 1824

Munch, Peter Andreas: Grönlands og Amerikas Opdagelse. *Almuevennen.* Aargang 2 Nos. 9-10, Christiania 1850, pp. 65-67
– *Det norske Folks Historie.* Christiania 1852-63

Næss, Almar: *Hvor lå Vinland.* Oslo 1954

Nansen, Fridtjof: *Nord i Taakeheimen.* Kristiania 1910
– *In Northern Mists.* London 1911
– The Norsemen in America. *The Scottish Geographical Magazine,* Vol. 27, Edinburgh 1911, pp. 617-32

Nielsen, Yngvar: Die ältesten Verbindungen zwischen Norwegen und Amerika. *Congrès international des Américanistes.* Vol. 14, Stuttgart 1906
– Nordmænd og Skrælinger i Vinland. *Det Norsk Geografiske Selskabs Aarbog,* Vol. 16, Kristiania 1904-05, pp. 1-41. Also in *Historisk Tidsskrift,* Ser. 4 Vol. 3, Kristiania 1905, pp. 248-93

Nordal, Sigurður: *Orkneyinga Saga.* Samfund til Udgivelse af gammel nordisk Litteratur, Copenhagen 1913-16

Nordenskiöld, A. E.: *Om bröderna Zenos resor och de äldsta kartor öfver Norden.* Stockholm 1883
– *Bidrag til Nordens äldsta kartografi vid fyrahundra års festen till minne om nya världens upptäckt.* Svenska Sällskapet for antropologi och etnografi, Stockholm 1892
– *Periplus, an essay on early history of charts and sailing directions.* Stockholm 1897

Nordland, Odd: Öya med giftarmåls-vanskane. *Viking,* Vol. 17, Oslo 1953, pp. 87-107

Norges Gamle Love

Nörlund, Poul: *Buried Norsemen at Herjolfsnes. An archaeological and historical study.* Meddelelser om Grönland, Vol. 67, Copenhagen 1924
– *De gamle Nordbobygder ved Verdens Ende. Skildringer fra Grönlands Middelalder.* Copenhagen 1934

Nörlund, Poul and Roussell, Aage: *Norse Ruins at Garder.* Meddelelser om Grönland, Vol. 76, Copenhagen 1930

Nörlund, Poul and Stenberger, Mårten: *Brattahlid* (Researches into Norse Culture in Greenland). Meddelelser om Grönland, Vol. 88, Copenhagen 1934

Ólsen, Björn Magnússon: Landnamas oprindelige disposition. *Aarböger for nordisk Oldkyndighed og Historie,* Copenhagen 1920, pp. 283-300
— Landnama og Eiriks Saga Rauda. *Aarböger for nordisk Oldkyndighed og Historie,* Copenhagen 1920 pp. 301-07

Olsen, Julius E.: *The Northmen, Columbus and Cabot, 985-1503,* New York 1906

Packard, Alpheus Spring: *The Labrador Coast. A journal of two summer cruises to that region.* New York 1891

Peschel, Oscar: *Geschichte des Zeitalters der Entdeckungen.* Stuttgart 1858

Pinkerton, John: *Modern Geography.* Vols. I-II, London 1802

Pohl, Frederick J.: *The Lost Discovery. Uncovering the track of the Vikings in America.* New York 1952

Raestad, Arnold: *Kongens Strömme.* Kristiania 1912

Rafn, Carl Christian: *Antiquitates Americanae.* Copenhagen 1837, Supplement, Copenhagen 1841

Ravenstein, G. E.: *Martin Behaim, His Life and Globe.* London 1908

Reeves, Arthur Middleton: *The Finding of Wineland the Good. The History of the Icelandic Discovery of America.* London 1890

Robberstad, Knut: *Frå gamal og ny rett.* Vol. I, Oslo 1950

Roussell, Aage: *Norse Building Customs in the Scottish Isles.* Copenhagen and London 1934

Ruge, Sophus: *Geschichte des Zeitalters der Entdeckungen.* Berlin 1881

Schöning, Gerhardt: (Snorri Sturluson) *Heimskringla.* Copenhagen 1777
— Norges Riges Historie, Vols. I-III. Copenhagen 1771-73, 1781

Shetelig, Haakon: *Vikingeminner i Vest-Europa.* Oslo 1933
— Grönland og Vinland. *Det norske Folks liv og historie,* Vol. I, Oslo 1930, pp. 363-71

Skånland, Vegard: Supplerende og kritiske bemerkninger til Eirik Vandvik: *Latinske Dokument til Norsk Historie fram til år 1204, Historisk Tidsskrift,* Vol. 41 No. 2, Oslo 1961, pp. 136-38

Smith, Charles S.: The Vinland Voyages. *Bulletin of the American Geographical Society,* Vol. 24 No. 4, New York 1892, pp. 510-35

Söderberg, Sven: Vinland. *Snællposten,* Malmö Oct. 30, 1910

Sölver, Carl, V.: *Vestervejen, Om vikingernes sejlads.* Copenhagen 1954

Sprengel, Matthias Christian: *Geschichte der Europaer in Nord-Amerika.* Leipzig 1782

Steensby, H. P.: *The Norsemen's Route from Greenland to Wineland.* Meddelelser om Grönland, Vol. 56, Copenhagen 1917

125

Stefánsson, Vilhjalmur: *Greenland*. New York 1947
— *Northwest to Fortune*. London 1960

Storm, Gustav: *Eiriks Saga Rauda og Flatöbogens Gröenlendinga-þáttr sampt Uddrag fra Olafs saga Tryggvasonar.* Copenhagen 1891
— Om Zeniernes reiser. *Det norsk Geografisk Selskabs Aarbog.* Kristiania 1891, pp. 1-22
— Söfareren Johannes Scolvus og hans reise til Labrador eller Grönland. *Historisk Tidsskrift*, Ser. 2 Vol. 5, Kristiania 1886, pp. 385-400
— Om Betydningen af 'Eyktarstaðr' i Flatöbogens Beretning om Vinlandsreiserne. *Arkiv for nordisk filologi*, Vol. 3, Christiania 1886, pp. 121-31
— Studier over Vinlandsreiserne, Vinlands Geografi og Ethnografi. *Aarböger for nordisk Oldkyndighed og Historie.* Copenhagen 1887, pp.293-372
— *Studies on the Vineland Voyages.* Christiania 1884-89
— Columbus på Island og vore forfædres opdagelser i det nordvestlige Atlanterhav. *Det norske Geografiske Selskabs Aarbog.* Kristiania 1893, pp. 67-85
— Review of Nordenskiöld: *Periplus. Nordisk tidskrift för vetenskap, konst och industri,* Stockholm 1899, pp. 157-61

Suhm, Peter Friderich: Forsög til en Afhandling om de danskes og norskes Handel og Seilads i den hedenske Tid. *Skrifter,* Det Köbenhavnske Selskab af Lærdoms og Videnskabers Elskere, Part 8, Copenhagen 1760, pp. 19-84

Sverdrup, Otto: *Nyt Land; Fire Aar i arktiske Egne.* Vols. I-II, Kristiania 1903

Swanton, John R.: *The Vineland Voyages.* Smithsonian Miscellaneous Collections, Vol. 107 No. 12, Washington 1947

Tanner, V.: De gamla nordbornas Helluland, Markland och Vinland. Ett försök att lokalisera Vinlands-resornas huvudetapper i de isländska sagorna. *Budkaveln,* No. 1, Åbo 1941
— Ruinerna på Sculpin Island (Kanayoktok) i Nain's Skärgård, Newfoundland-Labrador. Ett förmodat nordboviste från medeltiden, *Geografisk Tidskrift,* Vol. 44, Copenhagen 1941, pp. 129-55

Thalbitzer, William: Skrælingerne i Markland og Grönland, deres Sprog og Nationalitet. *Oversigt* over Det Kongelige Danske Videnskabernes Selskabs Forhandlinger 1905, Copenhagen 1905-06, pp. 185-209
— *A phonetical study of the Eskimo language based on observations made on a journey in North Greenland 1900-1901.* Meddelelser om Grönland. Vol. 31, Copenhagen 1904

– *Four Skræling Words from Markland in the Saga of Eirik the Red.* London 1913

Thór∂arson, Matthías: *Vinlandsferdinar.* Safn til sögu Islands og íslenzkra bókmenta, Vol. 6 No. 1, Reykjavik 1929
– *The Vinland Voyages.* Trans. Thorstina Jackson Walters. American Geographical Society, Research Series No. 18, New York 1930

Thorkelsson, Thorkell: Den islandske Tidsregnings Udvikling. *Aarböger for nordisk Oldkyndighed og Historie.* Copenhagen 1936, pp. 46-70

Torfason, Thormod: *Historia Vinlandiae, History of Ancient Vinland.* New York 1891

Tornöe, J. Kr.: *Lysstreif over Noregsveldets Historie.* Norges Svalbard- og Ishavs-Undersökelser, Meddelelser No. 56, with English summary, Oslo 1944
– Hvitserk og Blåserk. *Norsk Geografisk Tidsskrift.* Vol. 5 No. 7, Oslo 1935, pp. 429-43. Note from English translation by Michael Spender, *The Geographical Journal,* Vol. 89 No. 5, London 1937, pp. 552-56. See also Courtauld, A.: A Journey in Rasmussen Land. *The Geographical Journal,* Vol. 88 No. 3, London 1936, pp. 193-215
– Report on the expedition with the sealer Signalhorn to Eastern Greenland in the fall 1931. *Oslo Aftenavis,* No. 266, Nov. 18, 1931. See also *Aftenposten,* No. 418, Aug. 20, 1932
– *Early American History: Norsemen before Columbus.* Oslo 1964

Vandvik, Eirik: *Latinske Dokument til Norsk Historie fram til år 1204.* Oslo 1959, p. 64 and pp. 170-72

Vartdal, Hroar: *Bibliographie des ouvrages norvégiens relatifs au Grænland.* Skrifter om Svalbard og Ishavet, No. 54, Oslo 1935

Wheaton, H.: *History of the Northmen or Danes and Normans.* London 1831. French ed. Poul Guillot, Paris 1844

Winge, Herluf: *Grönlands Pattedyr.* Meddelelser om Grönland, Vol. 21, Copenhagen 1902

Wissler, Clark: *Archaeology of the Polar Eskimo.* Anthropological Papers of the American Museum of Natural History, New York 1918

Wormskiold, M.: *Gammelt og Nyt om Grönlands, Vinlands og nogle fleer af Forfædrene kiendte Landes formeentlige Beliggende. Det skandinaviske Litteraturselskabs Skrifter.* Copenhagen 1814, pp. 283-403

Wright, John Kirtland: *The geographical lore of the time of the Crusades. A study in the History of Mediaeval Science and tradition in Western Europe.* American Geographical Society, Research Series No. 15, New York 1925

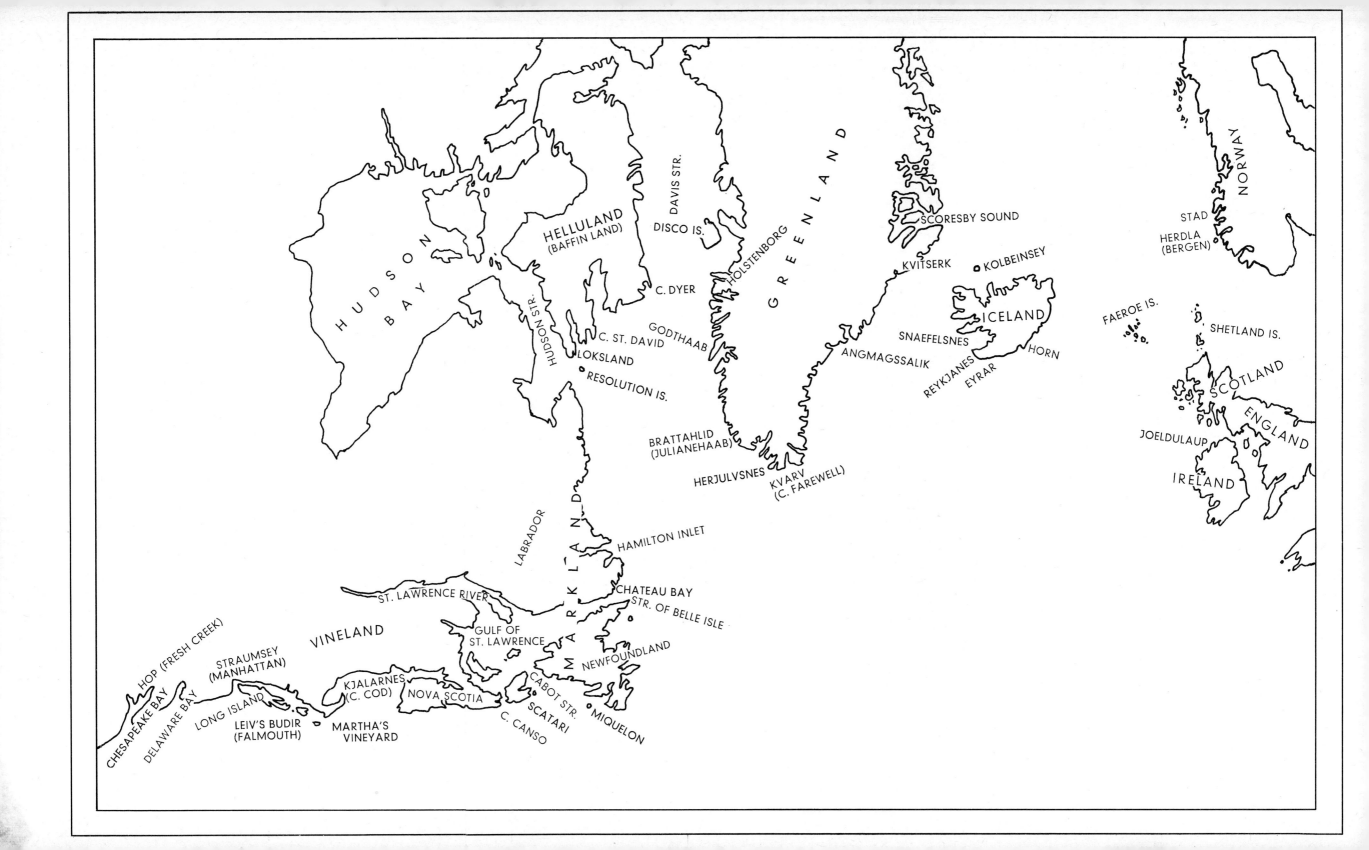